A truly heartfelt and endearing read

How to Rebuild Shattered Dreams is a thoughtful, inspiring guide on how to succeed in life and heal deep, emotional scars from the past.

Author LaRene Ellis (*Stones' Quest* series) details how she healed from her own troubled past and lives her dreams to the fullest. Abandoned as a young child, LaRene was tossed from one relative to the next, enduring abuse along the way. She not only survived, but is now thriving and sharing her story to help others.

In this book, LaRene explains how she recovered from the emotional and physical problems she suffered in her childhood through basic, yet very effective laws. She offers invaluable information on how to heal from emotional or physical abuse, how to program the mind to be successful, how to change old thought patterns and behaviors to live a healthy, vigorous life, and much more!

LaRene Ellis proves it's never too late to realize your dreams. This is truly a must-have for anyone seeking spiritual and emotional solace in life.

How to Rebuild Shattered Dreams

LaRene R Ellis

Gathering Place Publishers
Kaysville, Utah

Copyright © 2007 LaRene R Ellis. All rights reserved.

No part of this book may be reproduced in any form or by any means without permission in writing from the publisher.

Gathering Place Publishers, Inc.
P.O. Box 341
Kaysville, Utah 84037
SAN 256-0658

www.Rebuild-Shattered-Dreams.com

ISBN-10: 0-9754622-2-9
ISBN-13: 978-0-9754622-2-5

Edited by Jeff Curry
Designed and typeset by Marny K. Parkin
Cover by Benjamin Bair Ellis

Library of Congress Control Number: 2007907197

Printed in the USA
10 9 8 7 6 5 4 3 2 1

Dedicated to the man I called Jack. He saved my life and made it possible for me to learn the secrets of life. I'll always love him for being so supportive of my goals and me.

Contents

1	Introduction	9
2	Before the Dark Days	17
3	The Separation	29
4	New Places	41
5	Teenager	55
6	Finding Jack	65
7	Dying	87
8	I Found Me	99
9	Looking at a White Piece of Paper	105
10	I Found Love	115
11	Unpeeling the Layers	121
12	This Is What I Learned	127
13	Depression	135
14	Self-Worth and Love	143
15	How the Mind Works	151
16	How to Change a Core Belief	163
17	Laws That Govern Happiness	177
18	How to Handle Separation	189
19	Mastering the White Paper	195
	About the Author	203

Chapter 1

Introduction

"Timeout!" Jasper threw himself onto his bed. "I hate timeout!" He buried his head in his pillow. "I'm always the one who gets time-out! Buster never gets sent to his room. I think Mom likes him better than me. I'm seven years old. I'm not as young as he always treats me!" The pillow muffled his yells so he wouldn't get in more trouble, but he quickly found it hard to breathe. Rolling over, he looked around his room. The fleet of models that decorated his room looked crisp and invincible, but they didn't seem to care about his plight.

Stop . . . Wait . . . Let's stop right there. This book isn't a fictional story. It's a true story about my life. This book took me a year to find the courage to face my fears and write it. You're probably wondering why a person who could claim she knew how to rebuild shattered dreams would need courage?

This book is taking a tremendous amount of courage to write. Recently, something happened in my life, causing me to discover an unknown layer of scars. It was revealed to me when I started to promote my young adult series, *Stones' Quest*. I quickly learned how terrified I was to have strangers know about my past. Until then, no one ever asked me or knew how horrible my youth really was.

When I was a little girl, I was punished if I ever talked about what happened to me in my life. So when my PR man lined up some interviews for me to talk about my books on the radio, it came out during one interview that I had a layer of scars. Unbeknownst to me, I didn't know they existed.

The first interview was short and sweet. I rather enjoyed it. My second interview was terrifying and it wasn't their fault. The interviewer happened to trigger something from my past that I couldn't deal with in a split second. Her words caused me to clam up, not being able to speak. All she said was, **"You must've had a terrible life, growing up."**

It was very innocent and simple, but the fear of being punished because someone knew about my past made me unable to speak, forcing the interview to end abruptly. I had two other interviews and still struggled because I was afraid they would ask me about my past. They didn't mention it, but the fear was so strong. I could only answer with a yes or no. As you can see, I wasn't a very good interviewee. So I stopped the promotion until I could figure out how to overcome my fear of strangers knowing about my past.

Determined to overcome my fear, I heard about blogs and decided to put my life on the Internet to get used to people knowing about my past. I did receive a couple of nice comments and hoped I was done dealing with my fear. Then a publisher contacted me and suggested I turn my story into a book. Knowing how hard it would be for me to talk about my life, I thought about it.

After a month of thinking about my challenge, I decided to face my fear of past demons and do it. It was hard for me to admit I still found another area of scars that needed my attention. My motivation at first was to write the book, knowing how liberating it felt to face my fears and overcome them. Then I started to realize how much I understood and maybe people could benefit from my knowledge.

It isn't a complete autobiography. I've only talked about how my dreams were shattered so you could see how I rebuilt them. I was abandoned at the age of four and never again was I allowed to be a part of a family unit. My brother and sister were taken away and we all were forced to grow up alone. Neither one of us became a part of another family nor were we allowed to be a family unit even within ourselves. It feels strange to me to hear other people talk about going home. I always wonder what it would feel like. This was never an option given to my two siblings or me to be able to go back to a home or visit with people from our past, knowing we were a family.

From my story, you'll learn how I raised myself and what valuable lessons I learned from the experience. Since I had everything taken away, it allowed me to learn life's most valuable secrets. Life gave me something to compare the secrets against. As I think back, I wonder if it was possible to learn them in another setting. However, I cannot see how my life could've played out differently where I would still learn the secrets. For the record, I'm very appreciative of my unfortunate experiences. If I had to do it all over again, so I could learn what I did, my answer would be, **yes**.

My unfortunate experiences left me with some very deep scars. It would've been impossible to write this book if I hadn't overcome them first. To write this book, I had to revisit my deep depression, disappointments, and the degrading verbal remarks towards me. I had to revisit every ugly moment to make this book possible. I so appreciated what the younger me went through and the price I paid to find such wonderful secrets to life. I hope you appreciate it too. There was a very high price paid to make this book possible.

The purpose of this book is to reach out to others. Today, I see so many people confused and feeling so lonely. They are looking towards others or using medication to help make themselves feel better. They're asking others to give them what they need. One of the secrets to life is simple: **It wasn't ever meant to receive what you need from others**. They can't give it to you. It's impossible.

You are the only person who can give it to yourself. Just like Dorothy from the *Wizard of Oz*, you already have the ruby slippers on that can take you to anywhere you want. It isn't necessary to expect or wait for someone else to give you what you need.

After you learn the steps to rebuild your life and dreams, you can pick that kind of life you want. You can stop spending your life trying to deal with the scars others forced upon you. You can find joy that comes from the spirit out, affecting every aspect of your life.

I have spent over thirty-five years studying how to rebuild my shattered dreams. I read over two hundred books, listened to numerous positive-thinking tapes, and took classes in universities in search of knowledge. In my research, I learned a very interesting aspect that you might already know. We learn by **comparing**.

Let me share with you an example. One night, I watched Jay Leno on the *Tonight Show*. He had an animals segment with octopuses. Right there, they had my attention. I hadn't seen one in my life yet. So I watched thinking how ugly they were.

The trainer wanted to demonstrate how intelligent octopuses were. He had two live octopuses in separate clear tanks of water. They both were clinging on the same side of their tanks with long tentacles, watching the trainer. In a nearby bucket, he had live fish to keep their attention on him.

As the octopuses watched, the trainer explained one octopus was born in captivity and had been hand-fed his whole life. He had no idea how to kill live prey and couldn't live in the wild until they taught him how to take care of himself. The other octopus had recently been caught in the ocean. So he had the killing instinct and could take care of himself.

They had caught the wild octopus for the sole purpose of training the tame one to kill his prey. The trainer explained the octopuses were very smart and he wanted to demonstrate it on Jay's show. With his explanation ending, he reached in the bucket for a live fish and dropped it into the tank of the tame octopus.

The wild octopus followed the live fish and hung on the side of the tank, wanting to get to it, while the tame octopus stayed hanging on the side of the tank, watching the trainer. He was expecting him to give him killed food. Seeing the tame octopus wasn't going to move, the trainer removed the live fish and walked over to the other tank. The wild octopus followed him.

When he dropped the fish in the tank, the wild octopus fell on the fish before he quickly returned back to the side of the tank to see if the trainer was going to give him more fish. The tame octopus let go of his side and attached himself to watch the wild one. Now that the trainer had his attention, he dropped another live fish into the wild octopus' tank. Again, he fell on the live fish before he swam back to the trainer. The fish was gone.

When the trainer reached into the bucket for another live fish, both octopuses were watching and waiting to see what he was going to do. The trainer came to the tame octopus and dropped it into the tank. Instantly, the tame octopus fell upon the live fish. Quickly, he returned to the side of the tank, waiting for more food.

Everyone clapped and cheered to see how fast the octopus learned. We learn the very same way. You're always measuring yourself and experiences against someone. We get upset with others because they might use a different method to do something than us. All the time, we're comparing. Think about it or watch yourself and others. We learn by comparing.

How many of us promised ourselves that we wouldn't copy our parents' method of raising a child? When you became an adult, you suddenly found yourself repeating everything just like your parents. Or you'll ask yourself, how did my parents handle this situation? After you ask the question and remember, you might choose to handle it differently from your parents. Watch yourself. You'll check first to remember how your parents handled the situation before you decide how you're going to deal with it.

Like the octopus, we want to remember how our parents handled the same situation to compare how we want to handle it. You might decide to handle it differently, but you will compare first against what you saw.

We weren't given a manual when we were born. So we spend a lot of time trying to figure out how to make it work. If we don't learn how to get out of a negative situation and heal from the scars, we end up refusing to look at our past or ourselves. It can be disappointing to not have a manual on how to handle a broken heart. I felt my shattered dreams were unique and no one would understand or care.

Sometimes, it seems like other people don't care at all because they don't know what to do. They, too, are asking the same questions in their hearts. This is one of the reasons why other people can't give us what we need. They can't give you what they haven't experienced. There are also other reasons why they can't help you and we will talk about that later in the book.

Since I was raised to take care of myself, I made it my responsibility to heal my past and restructure my life. By me giving you the opportunity to compare your life to mine, it's my hope. You might believe it is impossible to remove ugly moments that stop you from having a wonderful life. Hopefully, you'll learn that you can remove scars and you're okay. So you can remove the fear, stopping you from stepping forward into the future with happiness in your heart.

Remember, the unfortunate experiences are important to you. They are what make you *you*. They will never leave you, but you can turn them into fertilizer to be used to create a beautiful garden in your life. Thus, you can have peace while retaining the valuable lessons from among the ugly moments of life. From them, you can become stronger.

I know every step I took to remove the scars and you can follow them if you want to do the same thing in your life. Soon, you can see how you can turn any unfortunate experience into an asset.

For some of you who are still questioning that we learn by comparing, I want to talk about another research study done with humans. They did the same thing with humans that I talked about with the octopuses. The goals of the researchers were to learn how people function in an unsure situation. Do they figure it out or do they watch others and copy them?

This study started out with researchers doing a blind study. They picked a park that had tall bushes close to a sidewalk. There was a park bench close by, so the researchers could wait for unexpected people walking down the sidewalk. When a naïve person appeared, the researchers behind the bushes started to yell for help and rustle the bushes.

The researchers sitting on the nearby bench ignored everyone while someone recorded people's behavior with hidden cameras. When the yelling started, the unsuspecting stranger stopped to look at the bushes. Before they moved off the sidewalk, they always looked over at the bench at the researchers relaxed and unconcerned about anything.

Unsure of what to do, they would look between the bench and bushes. When the people on the bench did nothing, they would continue down the sidewalk. Some people would run away. No one in the blind study looked behind the bushes.

They deemed from the research that when we aren't sure about how to handle a situation, we copy those around us. It angered me that they would say this and I didn't believe them. Determined to prove them wrong, I started to watch myself.

When I was in a situation in public that was new to me, I watched to see how I handled it. Every time, I looked to see how other people were dealing with the situation and I felt compelled to copy them.

Humbled, I started to watch other people to see if they did the same thing and to see if they watched other people as well. Every time, I could see them looking at others to understand what they were supposed to do.

After seeing it happen numerous times, I finally accepted the truth that we learn by comparing. So this is why I choose to go back to my life and talk about parts of it.

My journey begins . . .

Chapter 2

Before the Dark Days

My journey began on a cold, snowy day or night in the middle of the winter. We lived high in the Rocky Mountains and since no one told me about my birth, I'm going to assume that it was snowy and cold at the time. In my family, I was the fourth out of five children. Some of us had many years between our ages.

We lived on a dairy farm about five miles from Park City, Utah. Our place was a working dairy farm, which means we had milking cows, a few chickens, and a horse that no one was allowed to ride. It belonged to my grandfather, who had it there for those who milked the cows for him. As you have guessed, we lived with my father's parents on their dairy farm.

When I was born, my grandparents on my father's side didn't live on the farm with us. They happened to be living in New Zealand. When they returned, I was two. I remember watching them walk down the path to the house. They seemed sad to be home. Later, I learned how much they loved living in New Zealand. They returned because they also wanted to see their children and grandchildren.

At a moment's notice, my grandparents would stop what they were doing to show anyone their slides on their life in New Zealand. My grandfather loved the country and the people. A couple of times, people from New Zealand would stop and visit with them when they came to America. I grew up feeling like I lived there too, seeing their slides so many times and meeting people from the country. It's a beautiful place and I've enjoyed meeting anyone from New Zealand.

With them returning home, we went from having the whole house to three rooms within the house. It was a possible arrangement as the house had two kitchens. So we had a kitchen, living room, and one bedroom, making up the three rooms. The house had an upstairs. We did have access to one out of three rooms and the landing at the top of the stairs. My oldest brother, Harold, had the bedroom while my older sister, Jen, and I slept on a couch next to the banister on the landing. My other siblings, Mary and Bud, slept on the couch downstairs with our parents in the bedroom.

The house was very cold upstairs, since our only heat was a coal stove downstairs, and during the winter the temperature would drop below zero. To this day, I love the cold and the mountains. I'm grateful to have had the opportunity to see the Andes Mountains. They are my favorite mountains in the world and they're very breathtaking.

Maybe, my love for mountains is in the blood, since some of my ancestors came from Switzerland before they moved to Germany. While my other ancestors came from England and Copenhagen, Denmark, they were all used to cold weather. I appreciate my ancestors and what they sacrificed so I could be born in America.

Bud and I with Mimmie, our mother's mother.

While my grandparents were gone, Dad didn't work on his father's dairy farm as someone else did. We just took care of the house. My father owned and ran a feed and grain business a mile away from the farm. Mother stayed home and took care of us, which pleased me since I always felt loved and secure when around her. Another person I was happy to be with was my maternal grandmother on my mother's side. We called her Mimmie instead of grandma.

I loved Mimmie as much as I did my mother. She was quiet and beautiful in my eyes and if she asked me to do anything, I was pleased to do it because she asked. We had a deep connection with each other that I can't explain. I felt so lucky to have had both my mother and her mother as my relatives.

Myself, Bud, and Mother.

It wasn't just me who had deep love for my mother. Years later, when I would meet people who knew her, they would tell me how much they loved her. She had affected them the same way she did me. Mother had a way of communicating total acceptance and love for you. When anyone talked about my mother, they beamed and I could see the love for her in their faces. Knowing my mother, she did love them too.

Mother could do anything with style and grace when it came to using her hands. I heard she was a good cook, seamstress, and loved gardening. She made many things for others with her sewing ability. The only thing I have of hers are a few doll clothes that she had sewn for me using an old-fashioned peddle sewing machine.

Mamma loved music and studied the piano and organ for either sixteen or eighteen years. I loved to listen to her practice. I would walk two miles with her so she could practice the organ at the local church. Mother loved classical music and instilled the love for it in me by listening to her play it.

When I hear classical music today, it reminds me of her and I feel her love. She was my security blanket and she still is even to this day. In my heart, when I hurt, I'll find myself wanting to call out to her so she could put her arms around me. I imagine her telling me that I'll be okay.

Where we lived in the mountains, we had interesting wildlife. It was common to find garden snakes slithering through the grass, which would send me screaming to my mother's arms. Around larger rocks, I would find scales of larger snakes, but never saw them. They would have a great time eating mice with all the open fields we had. My grandfather had a couple hundred acres at the time.

The acres left us with a lot of places to explore and I loved it. Sometimes you could see elk, mule deer, porcupines, bobcats, red-tail foxes, minks, and hawks. When I wasn't exploring, I would love to lie on my back and watch the clouds pass by overhead. We were so high up in the mountains, the clouds seemed to be just above my head. They seemed so close, I felt like it was possible to almost touch them.

A good lightning and thunderstorm was my favorite thing. Since we were so close to the clouds, the thunder was so loud that you'd want to put your hands over your ears. During a thunderstorm, a bolt of lightning would cause the windows on the house to turn a bright yellow. It scared me at first and I became tired of feeling afraid. Innocently, I decided to embrace the fact that it happened, choosing to love it. When I did, I stopped being afraid. I didn't know then how important that philosophy can be in our lives. It brings happiness. Down the road, I had to relearn that principle.

My favorite thing to do was to climb a hill that was close to the barnyard. Sitting on top of the hill, I could watch the valley below. The hill was next to a main road through the valley. Along the road, tall trees hid the hill, reaching the same height of it. So I could sit there for hours and not be seen, watching people, hawks, and listen to meadowlarks. They are my favorite songbirds.

While there, I would sometimes make up stories in my head about what really happened years ago. Where we lived, history stated that the

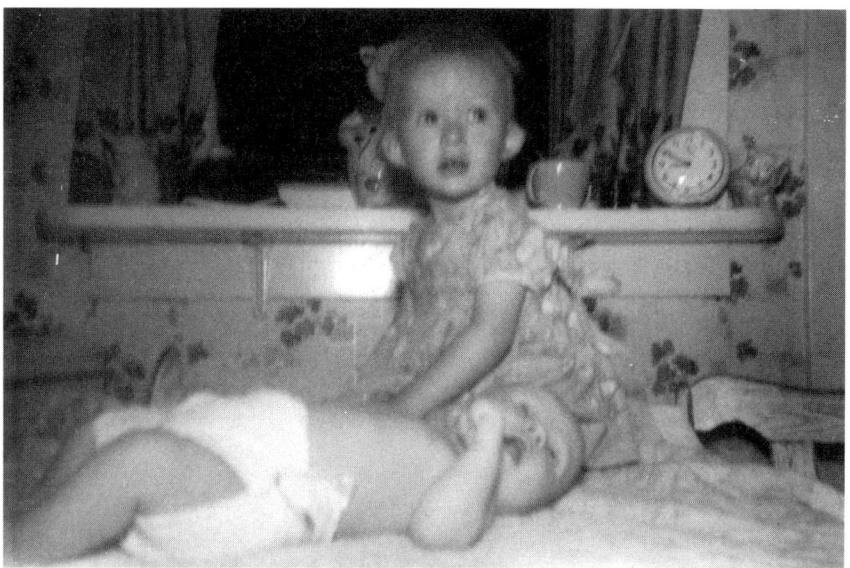

Bud and I.

Indians would stay in the valley during the summer. Western movies with John Wayne were popular as well as TV programs when I was a little girl. They probably influenced my stories about the small valley we lived in.

Another love I discovered was to walk along an irrigation stream that meandered through our place. Unless someone on a farm ahead of us had the water flooding their fields, there was always water in the ditch during the summer. So I would start at the milk barn, dropping a leaf into the water. Then I would follow the leaf to the end of our property. The stream would take me along fields and trees. It was so relaxing to watch my leaf bob up and down over the pebbles.

It started out being paper boats, but I learned quickly they wouldn't make it past the barnyard. Plain paper absorbs water quickly and I think it was my first scientific study. Now, I would like to spray the paper boat with hairspray and try it again. It would probably sink, but it would be interesting to see how long the paper boat would last compared to no hairspray on the paper.

Enjoying the solitude, I seldom invited my sister and brother, who were close to my age. Little did I know how much I would be by myself in the future and I would miss them. If I could do something over again, I would've spent more time with Bud and Mary. We all probably would've looked at things differently if we knew what was ahead of us.

In the meantime, life was good. In the summer, we seldom were inside. My sister, Mary, came up with a fun game that quickly became one of my favorites. She would take a comic book and we would each become a character. Mary would read to us about five pictures ahead. Then we would pick our characters and leave the comic book while we acted out a scene, ad-libbing.

Each one of us had a stick horse with a name. When we had finished with our ad-lib scene, we would ride our stick horses back to where Mary had left the comic book. Then she would read the next five pictures and we would continue acting out the story.

It was in our blood to love horses. With westerns being very popular on television and in the movies, we were at home. Our comic book was usually about Annie Oakley. If you don't know who Annie Oakley was, she was a woman who could stand in the saddle of her galloping

Mary, me, Bud, Dad, and Mother.

horse while she hit the bull's eye of a target with her gun. She was on TV for a while, along with Superman.

Mary was in love with Annie Oakley and she always had to be her. It was fine with me. Being asked to play the game, I felt privileged. We were riding our stick horses, pretending to be somewhere else, being someone else. I loved it and life was great.

We had our props and sound effects. Our guns were made out of wood. I think we did have one toy cap gun. With just one, sometimes, we would hit the caps with a rock to make the sounds of a gunfight.

When we wanted to make our riding horses look more realistic, we would cut young limbs from trees that still had their leaves on. So when we ran down the dirt cow trail, the dust would kick up like it does on a real horse. When the leaves fell off, we would throw the limbs away and start over. We always kept our other stick horses that had no leaves. They were our favorite horses.

Cousins were another fond memory I have from this past. I always looked forward to having my cousins come to the house. My mother was a twin and her other twin's kids feel more like sisters than cousins. There isn't a cousin that I don't like. I adore all of my cousins and feel lucky to have them, even though they were all older than Bud and I.

The few years I spent with my cousins, I have some wonderful memories. I'll never forget a cousin who was five years older than me. He showed me how to tie my shoes and I'll always adore him to this day for being so patient with me. It seemed so hard for me to understand how to tie my shoes.

I even adore my cousin who lived down the road from us. She lived a mile away and I felt sorry for her. My aunt Janice happened to be her mother and my father's sister. They lived a mile away on another dairy farm. Aunt Janice had two children, a boy and a girl. I never really remember spending time with the boy because he was twelve or fourteen years older than I was. His sister, Susan, was five years older than I.

So Susan was left without anyone to play with. I don't remember Aunt Janice ever allowing her to play with us at the house. When Susan and Aunt Janice did stop by the farm to visit with our grandparents, my aunt made Susan and her wear surgical masks. Aunt Janice was afraid that they might get something from us. I understood that she only wore the masks when we were around. So you can see why Susan never stayed and spent time with us.

The only time we could play together was when we went to her house. It wasn't pleasant to be in Aunt Janice's house and I doubt Susan was really happy. Yet, she wouldn't ever say it because she had nothing to compare her life to. At Aunt Janice's house, we weren't allowed to touch anything because our hands might be dirty. Even if we washed them, we were told the furniture was more important than us and not to touch it.

I've never met anyone with Aunt Janice's passion for things and image. My aunt loved music and would get upset if anyone performed better than she. Constantly, you would hear her tear everyone else down behind their back, while she stated how wonderful she was. This was my perception of her thoughts by listening to her numerous conversations.

Kids learn a lot about people around them because adults talk a lot in front of them. My father thought children were too stupid to understand what's going on around them. Children can understand. You might not know it because they struggle to express their thoughts clearly. Later, I'll show you just how much a child understands and how it affects their future.

Going back to my life, I had another love. It was to learn. I longed to go to school and use my mind. In my mind, I would picture getting off the bus and running to my mother, telling her about all the wonderful things I learned that day. This was a very important dream of mine at this time of my life.

Another dream I had was to be a part of a happy family, where I could feel secure and was wanted. This really was my biggest dream and I didn't realize how much I wanted it until it was taken away from me.

For some reason, my life started to change at the age of three, letting me know that my dream of a happy home was going to change as well. My parents started to fight constantly. When you're trapped in a three-room area, they couldn't hide it. Since I never talked to Mary and Bud at that time about it, I assume it was as hard on them as it was on me. Many times, I would put my hands over my ears to shut out my parents arguing. Inside, I wanted to scream for them to stop. It was miserable to listen to them constantly going at it. After a while, I learned to tune it out.

A year and a half before we were separated.

When my father wasn't around, my mother would be withdrawn and seemed to always worry. The only thing that seemed to stop their fighting was when I accidentally pulled the bookcase over on top of me. I just wanted to get something that was on top of it. Then there was the time I ran the sewing machine needle through my finger. It stopped them from fighting for a short moment.

It was only a couple of years ago when I was told why they fought. My father's only employee had embezzled seventy or a hundred thousand dollars from him. This was the fifties so you can see it was a lot of money for them. Until my father finally figured it out and sent the man to jail, they fought over the lack of money, not understanding the truth. My father took out his frustration on my mother, blaming her for spending all the money.

After he found out the truth, he became a very angry man and took it out on all of us. Now when I stand in his shoes, I can see he blamed himself for allowing his employee to run the front while he handled the grain. He shouldn't have trusted him to do the job right with the grain. My suspicions were my father never forgave himself. So he took his anger out on his family.

From my point of view, it seemed Mary got the brunt of his anger. There was nothing that she could do right. I always remember him yelling at her, calling her a liar. It was his pet word for all of us. After his experience with his employee, my father treated everyone in the family with distain. Everyone was guilty until proven innocent for being a liar.

Me, Jen, Mary, Mother, Bud, and Dad.

My father didn't want the truth. He wanted you to tell him what he deemed was the truth. It would change constantly so he could be superior in proving you to be a liar. When you told him the truth, he never accepted it. He wouldn't stop just there. My father would keep you there until you changed your story. So we would make up what we thought he wanted to hear. After we made up the story, he would accept it and then let us go.

He was so miserable to live with now. He stopped solely fighting with Mother and spread it all around. You never knew what was going to trigger his explosive behavior. We learned quickly during this time that we better tell him what he wanted to hear, if we didn't want to get hit. It was never the truth. You just agreed with where he was leading you with his words.

With the pressure of the lack of money, it changed my father into a different man. Finally, we had peace when he went to a hospital in Park City for what seemed to be months. I really don't know how long he was there and I really didn't care if he ever came home. My father went into the hospital to have his stomach removed.

When he returned, my mother became pregnant and extremely tired. The pressure of not having money only got worse for us. My oldest sister, Jen, became engaged at the age of sixteen. For some reason, girls in our area were getting married at the age of fourteen. So Jen wasn't considered young. Today, it makes me shudder at the thought, especially with what I know.

Harold, my oldest brother, was getting ready to go away to college. He worked for my grandparents on the farm so he could pay for his own schooling.

Jen's fiancé lived in California, so they had a six-month engagement with her living at the house. When Jen finally had her wedding, Mother was five months pregnant from what I understand. I just remember she wasn't feeling very well those days. After the wedding, Jen left for California with her new husband, Don. Harold left for college, leaving Mary, Bud, and I home with Mom and Dad.

I remember Mother spending a lot of time on the couch, lying down. While we played by her side, Father worked hard at the grain mill by himself. We were glad to have him gone so much because he still had this explosive anger after returning from the hospital.

In November, Mother started to get lumps all over her body. She went to see a doctor in Salt Lake and they put her in the hospital to run tests. To me, it seemed like a long time before I saw her again. When I did, it was only for a few minutes. What happened next isn't easy for me to talk about.

Our last Christmas with Mother.

Chapter 3

The Separation

It wasn't the same with Mother gone. Every night, the whole family, including my grandparents, would gather around her bed, kneeling down to pray for her. Bud and I didn't know what was really going on, since no one explained it to us. Mother was facing a life and death situation.

Everyone would take turns praying as they went around the circle. Bud and I would get bored and decided it was time to play. No one reprimanded us for playing during the family prayer, so we did it every time, thinking it was okay. I don't remember them telling us if Mother was coming home or not. We just assumed that she would always be there.

One day, our grandparents got us dressed to go into Salt Lake City. They said that we were going to visit our mother and that she was asking about us. All three of us were elated to finally be able to see Mamma. Excited, we all made pictures to give her. I remember being so excited to give her my present. We missed her so much.

I used flour glue and pasted a picture that I had cut from a magazine. I pasted it on top of the cover of a book she liked. Looking back, I wonder if Mary understood how serious the situation was at the time. Bud and I sure didn't know.

As we arrived at the hospital, the three of us were told to be very quiet. Apparently, she wasn't allowed out of bed like it was when we went to see our father. Mother was too sick and it felt strange to be paraded throughout the hospital while everyone stared at us.

In the fifties, children were never allowed anywhere in hospitals unless they were patients. It was a huge hospital in Salt Lake City so we had to wander through a lot of halls and floors.

Finally, we entered Mother's room. She was sitting up in bed. Tears came to her eyes as we ran to her. All three of us scrambled to get on her bed, wanting to get a much needed hug from her. However, to our dismay, Mother pushed us back, telling us to get off the bed. We reached out to her again and she refused to touch us.

Each one of us handed her our pictures, but she wouldn't touch them either. She just looked and nodded. We had never seen our mother act this way and it frightened me. It broke my heart when she told us to take our pictures home. Why didn't she want them? More important, why didn't she want us? The moment cut through our hearts like a knife. We all tried to climb up to her again, but she refused to have us on her bed. Stunned and dismayed, we left. I never wanted a hug so much as I did then and it never came.

It was a horrible experience for us all. I went home and ripped the picture off the book and washed it off so you couldn't tell it had ever been there. For me, I didn't want my mother to ever see it because I was so angry with her then.

Someone told me years later that she sobbed after we left. Mother wanted to hold us as bad as we wanted her to. The doctors made her afraid to touch us. In the fifties, the medical community had weird, cruel rules and they wouldn't even tell their patients if they were dying. Mother didn't even know what she had and it wasn't even contagious.

Mother had melanoma. It's a cancer of the skin that had spread all through her body, hitting her lungs last. Mother died never being able to tell us goodbye. And the three of us were never able to say our goodbyes to her as well. It was unfair to her as it was to us to not know the truth of her dying. She could've told others what she wanted them to do with us. Knowing my mother, I would strongly suspect that she would want us to stay together.

She left us a week later and we felt she didn't want or love us. No one cared to explain to us why Mother pushed us away. We did not have the communication skills to explain our pain, even if they refused to answer our questions. It was left for us to suffer through the lies and separation. We didn't receive closure and because of it, we all were deeply wounded.

My heart ached for my mother years after I had become a mother like her. It wasn't until I learned how to heal from that when I finally received peace. The pain never heals when the memory is attached to shock. We were shocked to learn our mother had died. These kinds of wounds do not heal on their own. You have to do something to heal them and you need to know what you're doing.

It would have been wonderful if someone could've talked to us about our feelings when we were kids. When we tried to talk about it, I was told it was wrong and that we shouldn't talk about how we feel. Unless someone asks a child how they feel, they usually don't say anything. We all need help to get through grief and loneliness at any age. During the fifties, children weren't considered important. So we were left to deal with the pain on our own and it never seemed to go away. Our open wounds made us feel very lonely and isolated. Each one of us thought we were the only ones who were hurting.

I remember the day so clearly when I was told my mother died. They handled it separately with each of us. With Bud, I don't know how he was told. He was only three. There were eighteen months between us.

Mary heard the saddest way in my opinion. With her sleeping on the couch, she overheard Jen, her husband Don, and Dad talking from the kitchen about Mother's death. Mary lay there crying, listening to their conversation. She was nine.

The next day, I was told. Jen took me by the hand and sat me on my grandparents' bed, while she went back to stand in the doorway. Bluntly, she told me that Mother had died and left. In shock, I remember watching Jen leave while I tried to internalize the information.

Today, I shake my head that my father put her up to telling us. It should've been him. We needed to hear that we were going to be okay and he was going to take care of us. Jen had no authority to tell me that I would be okay. My father's lack of support only terrified me more of him.

All I can remember my father doing during this time was whine about how he couldn't take care of us alone. When Jen's words finally sunk in, I fell to my grandparents' bed, sobbing. My dream of love and security was gone and I knew it. I never felt security or love again as a child.

Slowly, I curled up into a ball. At this moment, I said my first prayer from the depths of my soul. And I received an immediate answer. Warm, strong, invisible arms encircled me, while I cried out to them. How long was I there? I don't know. Those warm, invisible arms felt wonderful. In my heart, I knew the person holding me had felt my same deep pain before. He understood what it was like to be abandoned by those you love. His love permeated down to my soul and I'll never forget it.

The next time we saw our mother, she came to the house in a casket. We had the viewing at the house. Since the mortuary was so far away, it was customary to have the viewing at the house. I didn't like it. If they had any feelings for us children, they would have a viewing at the local church. At the same place, they had the funeral.

It was the same church where I met Shirley Temple a year later. She was an adult who came to put on a program for our small group of children that lived in the area. It was awesome to meet her and I'll never forget it.

Mother died in December, just two weeks before Christmas. It was the most horrible holiday to lose a parent. Christmas Day was so sad and dark with my father still whining about his situation. It wasn't until I was in my late thirties before I could start enjoying Christmas again.

At my mother's funeral, I remember meeting my great-grandfather for the first time. He was my mother's grandfather on her father's side. I remember that I came up to his knees as I looked up at him. Like Mimmie, he had an impact on me.

When he looked at me, I'll never forget the strength radiating from him. It was such a contrast from my father's whiney attitude. He had strength of faith and courage. In my heart, I wanted to go home with him. Feeling my father's insecurities, I wanted to go somewhere safe and be a part of their strength.

Mother's family drifted from our lives and I never really saw them until I was in my thirties. I found them again and learned my great-grandfather had died. Everyone told me stories about him. They always referred to and described him as a man with great courage and faith. When I heard about his life, I learned my first impressions were right about him.

It's important to learn about your ancestors. When I learned about him, I saw myself handling situations in their stories like he did. It gave me strength to know I could learn my way out of the darkness of my mother's death, which seemed to have a hold on me even as an adult.

Life seemed strange with everyone leaving us alone with our father after the funeral. Harold went back to college and Jen left for California. Unsure about our father, we watched him change. He stopped being angry and became moody. Our father would just sit and stare into space, refusing to interact with us.

With my father trying to dump his responsibilities on his parents, they stayed away. Our father had recorded Mamma's funeral and he would play it over and over again, wanting us to listen to it with him. When he turned it on, I would tell him it was dumb and I would go hide.

Our father didn't catch on what he was doing to us. Everywhere we went, he would tell every person he met, including strangers, "Don't you feel sorry for these children? They have no mother." They would look at us in horror and pity. I wonder what was going through their minds. Were they upset with what my father was doing to us or did they feel sorry for us because we had him as a father?

I would cringe to go anywhere with him. It embarrassed me and I was tired of being a person always wearing a label. It made me feel like I was a freak. You could hear people say we weren't going to amount to much because of our parents.

My whole life growing up, I was always introduced as the person with no parents. I was just living with this family for a while, but I had no future with them. My dream was to feel a part of someone's family and it never came. One of a human's basic needs is to feel like you belong somewhere. For the three of us, it never came and we felt so lonely and forgotten. Our needs didn't matter to anyone, including our own father.

To add to our self-image, we were a class of society that was called **the throw-away children.** We didn't have value and we were there only to be preyed on. With no one to protect us, people could do whatever they wanted to us and they did. Today, I see the same attitudes among undeveloped countries. Educated countries understand children are their future and you need to cherish them.

One day, I awoke to find my father angry. Listening to his words, someone in the town wanted Bud to come and live with them. Our father wouldn't hear of it. Why, I don't know. Bud would at least have a family's support and love. I think he was afraid that they would adopt him. All of us needed to be in a loving family that we could be a part of for the rest of our lives. Our father never gave it to us.

When our father was home, he ignored us. He would go off to work and leave us alone for hours. It would be midnight sometimes before he would ever come home. Our father didn't want the responsibility of raising us and we heard him say it numerous times.

Sometimes, he would talk about different people within the family that he could send us to. All the time, he always looked over the fence, wanting someone to rescue him from his sentence to take care of us. My father missed out on so many wonderful blessings by not taking care of us. He never got remarried. Not realizing, he would've been an attractive catch if he had kept us together, enjoying the process of being with us. Women like a man who takes responsibility. Since he didn't take care of us, they would've questioned his ability to take care of them. Most women had families.

During this time, I prayed a lot throughout the day. I would cry out for comfort and every time my prayers were answered by feeling the invisible, strong, warm arms around me. Each time, my love for those warm, invisible arms deepened. From this experience, I received a burning testimony of the power of prayer. It was the only way I survived what came next.

Instinctively, I knew from my prayers that Mother had left for a purpose. In my heart, I knew that I had agreed to it before she died. Life doesn't give you something that you can't handle. I accepted that my lifelines were the invisible arms that would come when I prayed.

Summer came and things hadn't changed with my father. Mary fought with him, trying to get him to respond to our needs and us. During the summer, Harold returned to run my grandfather's farm. Then, next fall, he had made the decision to move to Canada.

During this time, one day, I was standing in front of my mother's piano. My father was sitting in her rocking chair, staring at nothing. I missed hearing my mother play one of her classical pieces. Somehow, I wondered if I touched the keys, the piano would magically play one of her pieces one more time.

However, all I heard were a few plucks of the keys by my hand. Disappointed, I started to cry. Before I knew it, my father picked me up and brought me back to the chair in his arms. Rocking, he just held me. We both cried silently. I finally spoke and stated, "I miss her." He answered, "I do, too." After this moment, he never took me into his arms again.

It seemed like a couple of days later when he brought us all into the kitchen and said that he was going to leave us. Without a woman around, he felt like he couldn't take care of us and said that he was going to get cancer like Mother did. He said it was going to happen soon. Our father did die of cancer, but it was thirty-four years later.

To add salt to our already open wounds, he divulged that no one wanted us. So, he didn't know what would happen to us. This is just what children needed to hear, being the age of ten, five, and four. All he could say was good luck, leaving the room.

Fear consumed me, not knowing what was going to happen to us. The fear was so strong that I would wake up shaking in the morning. I almost dreaded going to sleep at night because I would dream about not knowing what was going to happen to me. It's such a daunting reality having to be totally dependant on others when they didn't want you.

During the day, I could shove it to the back of my mind. At night, the fear consumed my thoughts. The only way I would stop shaking was to pray. So I learned to pray every night. Every time, I could feel the invisible, warm arms holding me until I would stop shaking. Somehow, the arms gave me the courage to get out of bed again.

My father didn't leave the house immediately. He hung around, expecting to get sick. Getting tired of it all, I took my life into my own hands. My father would point to a house when he drove me to school that belonged to his cousins. He talked about the fact that they might take me in. So I decided to find out.

So one day, I got off at the school bus at their house and knocked on the door. I introduced myself and asked if I could stay with them. They called my father and I moved in. I spent most of my first grade with them. They always made sure my hair was done for school and I had nice clean clothes. The woman always played with us. They had one son who was a year older than me that they had adopted. I liked it there. After my birthday, I started to miss Mary and Bud and I wanted to go home to them.

After talking to my father's cousins, they sent me home. I went home only to find Bud was there. Mary was gone and my father was gone. Mary had left shortly before I arrived home.

My father had gone to California for about six months, leaving Bud with my father's parents. It upset me that Mary was gone and I didn't know about it. My father seldom visited me at his cousins' house. In a way, I felt that it was my fault that she left. Maybe, if I had stayed home, she would still be there.

With it being just Bud and I with our grandparents, I got to know my father's parents who lived in the other part of the house for the first time. By getting to know my father's parents, I started to understand why my father appeared to be so emotionally immature.

I guess even at this young age, I was a writer. I always wanted to know the background of everyone around me, so I could learn why they behaved the way they did. So I'm going to describe the personalities of the people around Bud and myself.

My grandmother was dark. She seldom smiled and wasn't a warm person, unless she knew you. When my mother was alive, we had the only telephone in the house. Every time Mother was outside in the garden, my grandmother would come over to our side of the house to use the phone. She would call Aunt Janice who lived down the road and they would talk until my mother came into the house. The minute my mother stepped out, Grandma would come back in and talk with Aunt Janice.

This was where I saw a side of my grandmother that she had kept hidden from most people. She didn't mind talking in front of Bud and me. She would disparagingly talk about our parents. Remember, Aunt Janice was the person who would visit us, wearing surgical masks so we wouldn't contaminate her and her daughter.

Listening to my grandmother's conversations, I understood why Aunt Janice held herself up to be better than everyone around her. She was taught to think that way by her mother. Grandma had two lists that she separated the people around her into. You were either on her bad or good list. There wasn't anything in between the two. If you were on the good list, it meant you were perfect and you had to be perfect. If you were on the bad list, you were considered evil. She would only have one person on the good list at a time, and I thought that was interesting. In my research, I found out why and I'll explain it to you later.

My grandmother had three children and it was obvious that my father and his sister were on her bad list. They were the evil ones. Aunt Janice was the youngest and always had to be perfect. My grandmother didn't ever do this openly. It was done behind closed doors and in secret. She even kept it from my grandfather. When she thought no one was around, she opened up her true self and it was ugly. Secrecy was very important to her.

When my grandmother was on her deathbed, she told my father how much she hated him. I don't know if she did it to his sister too. With Aunt Janice not living too far away, Jen grew up around her. My sister, Jen, told me that she idolized Aunt Janice. They were close until Harold became old enough to work for them. Then she ignored my sister. Somewhere in Jen's childhood, she made a decision to be like Aunt Janice.

Little did I know by living with my grandparents, she would separate both Bud and I into the two groups. When no one was around, she would call me the evil one and I never heard her use that name with Bud. One day, Bud and I came in laughing while we entered the room. With my grandfather outside working, she pounced on me, backing me into the corner. The whole time, she screamed at the top of her lungs, ripping into me on how evil I was.

During that moment, the invisible arms surrounded me, whispering into my ear that I shouldn't believe it. Now, I was only six years old and my protection wouldn't allow me to believe it. With the protection, He allowed me to really see what was going on around me.

You're probably wondering what happened to my grandmother to make her so emotionally unbalanced. When I became an adult, my grandmother became the first person I researched. What in the world happened to this woman? It had to be interesting.

I learned she had been deeply hurt as a child by her father. Her parents divorced against their wills, soon after she was born. When she got to know her father, he was married with more children from another marriage. For some reason, he acted like he didn't know who she was. Yet, she saw him all the time because they lived in a small town.

When I stepped in my grandmother's shoes to learn how she felt, I saw she was deeply crushed. Her mother never remarried and my grandmother blamed herself for her father not acknowledging her. Somehow, she was labeled as being evil. She could've easily given that label to herself.

Understanding the whole story, I stood in her father's shoes and learned he deeply loved her. In those days, fathers weren't taught to express their love to children, let alone one he wasn't allowed to claim as his daughter. My grandmother could only love one child because she was an only child.

I never hated my grandmother. In fact, I never hated anyone. It was easy to be angry with others, but I never crossed the hate line. In my heart, I knew the invisible arms wouldn't come to me when I prayed to be comforted, if I had crossed that line. He was my lifeline. It was hard to live with my grandmother because of her abusiveness. I needed Him to stay alive.

Where there is darkness, you'll find light. I loved my grandfather and he was my first love. He was my hero because just his presence protected me from my grandmother's hate and anger. Seeing him come into the house, I felt like a puppy wagging its tail. He was a tease and he had a gift in telling a story that kept you captivated. I loved to be around him and loved how he treated my grandmother. You could tell he loved her. I never saw that in my father. Again, my father couldn't give something that he never felt from his mother.

My favorite day of the week was Sunday. It was a day I could spend with my grandfather. In the summer, he would go outside and park his car underneath a tree that would overlook our tiny valley. Then he would climb into the front seat and read. I insisted on joining him and he always seemed perplexed by it.

I loved to be around him and I was afraid to be alone with my grandmother. So I would sit in the backseat, watching the comings and goings of people. We had a great view of different farms around the valley and I stayed quiet, pleased to be in his presence.

The other time I was allowed to go with him was when he would go fishing. He loved to fly-fish and it was beautiful to watch. I'd stay on the edge of the river, watching him wade out into the water. It was never anything that I liked to try, but I did enjoy watching it.

Since we are talking about grandparents, I mentioned before that I worshiped my grandmother Mimmie. When I became an adult, I learned that she had asked for me to come and live with her. The news filled a hole for me. Someone truly wanted me because they loved me.

It also made me furious that no one told me when I was a child. I needed to know then, not as an adult, that she wanted me. Even if I didn't go with her, it would've eased the pain in my heart from our father saying that no one wanted us.

One reason I didn't know about it was that I never saw Mimmie after the summer of Mamma's death. She died almost a year after my mother did and no one told us about it. Eventually, I heard Mimmie had died and it hurt not to be able to attend the funeral. Everyone thought it would be too hard on us. Again, we had no closure. All three of us were kept in the dark. If I had my choice, I would've gone. It would've given me another chance to know my mother's family. Maybe, someone would've dispelled the lies that were being told to us.

It might have helped the three of us get some closure in regards to feeling like our mother didn't want us. All three of us were frozen in the moment of learning about our mother's death and our mother pushing us away. Since we received no reassurance that we were loved, we stayed in this frozen state of fear, loss, and guilt.

In my fictional series, *Stones' Quest,* I show how the characters handle their traumatic moments in their lives. I explain how they rebuilt their shattered dreams and find peace and joy by using the principles that I'm talking about in this book.

At the same time, you're being entertained with adventure, suspense, mystery, and romance. The protagonist has to deal with inner demons while he unravels the secret to what started the civil war and to find the powerful Master Stones that can stop the war and bring peace to the galaxy and heal his life.

I wrote it for the ten to seventeen year olds, in case there was someone else out there who went through what I did as a child. Maybe, they would see an example of how to handle their lives properly.

Chapter 4
New Places

Every person's life isn't totally dark every minute. Even though our grandparents didn't hug us and communicate their love for us, our grandmother did do some nice things at times. She read stories to both Bud and me. This is where I think my love for stories and books evolved. My favorite stories came from *Grimm's Fairy Tales*. Today, I wish I could hear her voice reading to me. She did it almost every night after we were tucked into bed. When we moved away from the farm, Grandpa would spend time reading to us the complete story of *The Wizard of Oz*.

Eventually, we moved away from the farm and moved to a house in a nearby town farther away from Park City. Grandmother seemed a little happier here. She was close to one of her half sisters and other friends. We stayed here while I went to the second grade. It was okay living there, but I missed the field and places to go exploring. Here, I had to deal with people within an unhappy small town.

When Mary left, I seldom saw her again. Mary quickly became an acquaintance to me. Let me tell you about Mary and what happened to her. Jen and her husband came back from California with a new baby. They were the ones who asked her to come and live with them in Salt Lake City.

With Mary leaving in March, I didn't hear much about her until six months later. In September, my father showed up at his parents' house, upset. He had returned from California and was living in Salt Lake.

Mary was ten or eleven. I'm not sure. Salt Lake City was a good two-hour drive from us. During the summer, Jen and her husband, Don, started to leave her alone for the whole weekend to go visit Don's family. Therefore, Mary was left alone to fend for herself.

Feeling lonely and frightened, she started to invite her friends over for a slumber party, not telling them why. When the parents came to pick up their kids, they learned that Jen and Don weren't home. They had left Mary alone and it happened regularly. The neighbors got concerned about Mary's welfare and they got my father involved. This was why he was so angry. He couldn't believe that Jen would do this to Mary.

Jen and Don told Mary that they were going to have me come and live with them. She was excited, thinking we would be able to live together again. Shortly afterwards, Jen told her that she had to leave. School had just begun. When Mary told her friends at school that she was leaving Jen's house, neighbors got involved.

One neighbor invited Mary to come and live with them. I do know from what my father told my grandparents that things became very ugly for Jen and Don. Having enough, they moved from the area. They were renting month to month so it would've been easy for them to pick up and go.

It upset me that Mary didn't come back and live with us, so my father took me to see her. I don't remember Bud going with us. It did help me to see Mary was happy and well taken care of. Mary stayed there for a number of years before her life changed again. The mother in the family died suddenly and the family asked her to leave.

I don't remember exactly where she went next. All I knew about Mary was she went to four different families. After spending a couple of years with them, one of the parents would die and they would ask her to leave. This happened until she went to college.

Today, when we talk about what the two of us went through, I think her life was harder than mine. Since she knows first-hand what I went through, Mary tells me my experience was a lot harder. Everywhere she went, the people treated her with respect and didn't use her to benefit themselves. Bud and I weren't that lucky. The fact was all three of us had very hard lives and didn't enjoy much of a childhood.

At the age of seven, I had a major change enter my life. There was something about the age of seven with Bud and me. Our lives drastically changed at seven. Jen came to our grandparents' house and asked me if I would like to spend the summer with them. Sure, I thought. I would get an opportunity to know a sibling. Jen promised I would be able to come back for school and it was only for the summer.

So I packed up a few things and left for a great adventure. My grandparents didn't say much to me about it. So I don't know how they felt about me leaving. When I arrived at Jen's house, she had two children who I hadn't seen before. They both were in diapers. It had been two years since they had Mary come and live with them and I wasn't too concerned since I was only visiting for the summer.

Jen lived in Salt Lake City and she made sure I got to know all the different kids that were in the neighborhood. There were quite a few girls, especially those who were close to my age. The summer at Jen's was fun.

She went out of her way to make sure I had fun and I deeply appreciated it. For the first time, my pain of our mother being gone seemed to ease. Jen made sure that I felt a part of her life and she truly enjoyed being with me. Finally, I wasn't being treated like a stray dog. This is how I felt with my grandmother and I didn't realize it until I had something to compare it with.

We went to Yellowstone and did some camping. It was the best three months of my life that I had ever spent so far. So when Jen came and asked me if I wanted to stay with them permanently, I didn't hesitate.

It was August and soon after I agreed to stay, our father showed up to talk with Jen. He ignored me, which was fine. I hadn't seen him all summer and we saw very little of each other after I left to go live with his cousins. After a long discussion, our father left without saying much to me.

Shortly, I learned what took place in their meeting. My father had sent me a letter with some cash in it. Jen and Don wanted him to pay for taking me into their house. Plus, he was going to pay for all of my clothes, medical care, and any extra activities. My grandparents paid for my Christmas and I think they gave them money for my birthday. I don't remember getting anything much more than pencils or paper. Jen and Don wouldn't be putting out a penny on me and they never did.

My father agreed to it and laid out the financial agreement in the letter so I wouldn't ask him for any extra money. Knowing my father, he didn't trust Jen to tell me and he was right. They never told me and I don't know if they knew my father had told me. For some reason, I still have the letter.

So I went back to my grandparents' home and packed my things. Soon after, Jen changed. She started to treat me like our grandmother. Jen became dark and moody, seldom talking with me for fun. She stopped playing with me, not caring if I was having fun.

During the summer, Don had stayed quiet and ignored me. Now, he changed too and it wasn't pleasant. He started to become sarcastic and rude with me. Like my grandmother, he had pet names for me and didn't mind calling me by them when neighbors, my father, or friends weren't around.

By listening to them talk, I learned that they had financial problems and I was a job for Jen. Don acted like he resented the fact that they had to bring me in so they could make an extra income.

On top of them being paid, Jen and Don gave me jobs to do around the house. He would always tell me that it was the least I could do, since he allowed me into the house. My first job was doing dishes. I did them seven days a week. As the family grew, it would take me two hours to wash them and it didn't matter what I needed to do.

Quickly, I got the point that I was there to work for them. Don and Jen would constantly threaten me to never talk about what happened behind their doors to other people. They made me feel very fearful of them and I became afraid of telling anyone how miserable my plight was at home. Just like Grandmother, secrecy became very important to them.

As I aged, jobs were piled on. All my friends were babysitting and I started to do it for them. Everyone was getting paid twenty-five cents an hour. My friends would talk about how much they were making, so I kept track so I could talk about my babysitting money.

When it reached eleven dollars, I finally asked Jen when I was going to get paid like my other friends. To my dismay, Jen told me they had no intention of ever paying me. It was why I was there. It broke my heart to hear from their mouth that I was there for them to use and they didn't want me to be a part of their family.

In my heart, I kept hoping it wasn't true. I finally got the point that I didn't matter to them when I made a Mother's Day card at school. Excited to have the opportunity to give, I gave the card to Jen. In anger, she shocked me by yelling at me like our grandmother did. "I'm not your mother! Don't you dare ever give that to me again!"

Crushed and finally understanding my role in their lives, I felt the warm, invisible arms around me. Staring at the card, I decided to throw it away. Then I remembered an elderly lady who lived across the street alone. I felt compelled to go see her with the card. Not knowing what I was going to say, I knocked on her door. When she opened the door, I handed her the card and said, "I didn't think you would get a Mother's Day. I didn't want you to feel left out." She beamed and took the card, thanking me.

I learned a very valuable lesson that day. When you give service, it eases your pain. Going home, I had my pain increase. With each day, Don became worse with his verbal abuse. At the time, Don Rickles, an up-and-coming comedian, started to become popular. Don really liked him and I did too.

Don Rickles' style of comedy was to roast someone in the audience or another celebrity. Don decided to copy him, thinking it was funny and cute. It didn't take me long to put the two together because he would talk about mirroring Mr. Rickles.

Every night, Don would come into the house and read his newspaper before talking to anyone. When he finished, he would start in on me, copying Don Rickles' style. He would call me disparaging names with a lot of sarcasm and anger. What Don didn't understand about Mr. Rickles was that he always showed love to the people he roasted afterwards. So they knew he truly liked them.

Jen's husband never let you know that he cared. The anger in his tone made it miserable to live with. I lost respect for him because of it. To me, it felt like he was unleashing his anger for his life on others and in my eyes he looked ridiculous most of the time. It was unacceptable behavior to treat anyone this way. Verbal abuse, like this, cuts into the heart and it doesn't heal. A physical wound at least seals up.

When I mentioned it to Jen, she would just shrug her shoulders. She delivered the message that my feelings didn't matter and they were unimportant to her. About five years ago, she asked me why I didn't like her husband.

I brought up how abusive he was. She just shrugged her shoulders and stated, "He treated me the same." Again, she still doesn't get it. She delivered the message that my feelings didn't matter. Jen had her own problems. If she would've said that he did it to her and knew how much it hurts, it would have been better. It made me wonder if Don threatened her too about talking about his abuse.

Resigned to my fate, I went back to waking up in the middle of the night, shaking. I sent letters to my father, requesting that he come and remove me from Jen's house. He never responded to me. When he would talk with me, the only thing he would say was, "Don't get attached. You'll never know when I'm going to move you."

I don't know if he did talk to Jen about it. If he did, I guess Jen lied about what was going on in the house. Nothing changed and he refused to ever talk to me about it when I brought it up with him. Years later, he gave me all my letters back and I have them too.

With no one reining Don in, he only got worse. Feeling trapped and alone, I started to become consumed with depression. Each night, I prayed to stop breathing. I was too young to understand suicide, so I prayed that someone else would take my life and end my misery.

Every dream I ever had was dashed. So far, I learned if something wonderful happened to me, then I would be punished by my life becoming worse. Many times, I would cry myself to sleep, pleading to die during the night. When I woke up to find I was still alive, sometimes I would cry again.

During the summer, I requested to go see Bud and my grandparents. Maybe, I could go back. When I returned, I found Bud's life like mine. We were only eighteen months apart. With him close to turning seven, he went to live during the summer with Aunt Janice. She wanted him to work on the farm.

When I saw his living conditions, I was horrified. Aunt Janice had always disappointed me in the past. She embarrassed me when she would come to the house with her surgical mask on her face. Now, she really had gone too far.

Aunt Janice had three bedrooms in her house. Susan, her daughter, lived at home, but her brother didn't. I think he was married. When I asked Susan why Bud lived downstairs, she told me that Aunt Janice was afraid he would contaminate her brother's room in case he visited.

Bud had to sleep in the basement. Let me describe this basement to you. It was totally unfinished, except for one room. In this room, my aunt had her food storage and a clothesline. You could always find her two mink coats hanging in the room. In one corner, she had a washtub. If she didn't hang clothes outside, they were hung in the basement. I don't know if that caused the basement to stink or it was because of the open shower, toilet, and sink. They didn't have walls and you showered on the cement because nothing else was finished.

Along with the smell, the basement was dark and dingy with tiny windows lining the top of the cement walls. They were never opened. My uncle had to enter the house through the basement and shower before he came upstairs. It was the same for Bud. He was allowed to eat in the kitchen, but he had to sleep in the basement.

My aunt hung blankets around his bed to give him some kind of walls. The only thing I remember was a dresser drawer and a bed. They placed the bed underneath a light bulb with a string so he could reach it. At the foot of his bed sat his toys that Grandmother happened to be showering him with. It made me wonder if it was her way to ease her guilt for Bud's living conditions. He was so busy that some of the toys were still in their original package.

I could see that my situation wouldn't be much better if I returned. For some reason, Grandmother, Aunt Janice, and Jen treated us like stray dogs and didn't think it was unacceptable to use us.

Going home, I gradually found my life getting worse. With me being able to baby-sit, Jen started to ground me for everything. When I got older, I caught on to her lies and I got punished longer for pointing them out.

Quickly, I started to learn that Jen made up in her mind that she had to appear like a wonderful parent and person. When people came to the house, they would comment that she was so wonderful because she had taken me in. Never did Jen or Don tell them that my father was actually paying them to take care of me. They would twist the story so they would look like these wonderful people.

They lied sometimes about grounding me so I could stay home and baby-sit. Listening to them talking, they didn't want anyone to think they were abusing me. I had brought it on myself and this was why I always had to stay home when they wanted to go somewhere.

To prove how wonderful of a parent she was, Jen started to tell me what I could wear. She made me wear the same clothes all week so it didn't increase her having to wash clothes. They didn't get praised for what they did with their own children, so I don't remember them making their kids do it.

I've never seen anyone so starved for praise as Jen and Don were, even if they had to lie just to get it. Today, I don't understand it unless they were addicted to the emotion of praise. It is possible to become addicted to chemicals your emotions create. We will talk about this later.

The point is I felt like I didn't have a true carefree childhood. To put on a show, they would sometimes allow me to go swimming with my friends. But if they went to an ice-cream shop afterwards, their parents would always have to bring me home before they went. They had ridiculous curfews. I didn't have to go to bed early, but I had to be home at an early hour.

The nights were the worst for me. During the day, you had things to distract your pain. At night, there was nothing and I dreaded it. The stress and fear of what I had to endure became more than I felt like I could handle. Anxiety and depression consumed me. Many nights,

I would cry myself to sleep. I had lost my hope and felt trapped in a miserable situation.

My prayers increased, pleading Him to stop my breathing during the night. My heart was so broken and I was so tired of being used and unwanted. Fear had consumed me with no one coming to my rescue to protect me. Seeing every morning I was still alive, my thoughts went back to what I did after my mother's death.

There was a Golden Book my mother had bought called *God*. Lovingly, I would run my fingers over the pages. Every time, I felt the same love I received from being in the invisible arms. Somewhere in the moving around, the book became lost or it was thrown away. I don't know what happened to it. The book gave me peace when I held it and I felt compelled to find it again.

At Jen's house, I desperately wanted to search for something to replace it. Rummaging around the house, I happened to place my hand on a book. Instantly, I felt the warmth of the invisible arms. It gave me the same feeling I had with my book on God, but it was stronger. Picking up the book, I realized it was an adult version of the book, thicker with no pictures. The book touched me in such a way that I struggle to use the right words to express it. The book seemed to soothe my broken heart and I felt peace just holding it. Today, the book is still in print by Random House and I've read it numerous times.

Without asking anyone, I took the book to bed with me, holding it tightly against my chest. While holding it, I prayed that He would end my life. Peace consumed me while I fell asleep, making it through the nights. In the mornings, I would slip the book underneath my pillow, feeling the courage to make it through one more day. I'm very appreciative of the book as it removed my nightmares.

The book lived underneath my pillow without anyone knowing about it. I changed the sheets on my bed, so it was safe. This time, I didn't mind changing my own bed, since I didn't want Jen or Don asking me about it. The book was keeping me alive and I didn't want anyone taking it away from me. It was my only source of love, acceptance, and strength.

I appreciated my guardian angels that always looked after my safety. One day while I was washing dishes, I did something very dumb. Looking back, I should've known better since I was in the fourth grade. Out of ignorance, I sat the base of a blender, without the glass top on the machine, and turned it on. My goal was to see what the blades looked like spinning around.

Instead of the blades spinning around, it flew off the base, heading for the glass backing on Jen's new stove. In fear of Jen punishing me, I decided to stop it from hitting her stove. Right before I reached out to stop it, I heard in my mind, If you're going to stop it, you need to grab it on the bottom.

Confused, I wasn't quite sure how to grab the bottom. In panic, my hand went over the top of the twirling blades and it fell to the stovetop. I screamed as blood went gushing everywhere. Looking back, it was the sight of all the blood that caused me to scream. I don't remember the pain.

It took hours for the doctor to stitch me up. He kept shaking his head and repeated, "This is a miracle." The blades cut perfectly around my tendons in my fingers, but also sliced into the bone. It took over a hundred stitches to sew my hand up. I stayed awake, watching the doctor place every stitch in my hand.

In my heart, I knew my guardian angels had saved my hand. At least someone cared about me, keeping me as safe as possible. I very much appreciated to be a part of that miracle. As I grew older, I learned others had experienced those invisible arms and miracles in their lives. If you haven't read it, I would like to share it with you.

Everyone has probably heard of the poem called "Footprints." For those of you who haven't heard of or read it before, or wish to read it again, I have placed it below:

> One night a man had a dream. He dreamed he was walking along the beach with the Lord. Across the sky flashed scenes from his life. For each scene, he noticed two sets of footprints in the sand: one belonged to him and the other to the Lord.
>
> When the last scene of his life was flashed before him, he looked back at the footprints in the sand. He noticed that many

times along the path of his life there was only one set of footprints. He also noticed that it happened at the very lowest and saddest times in his life.

This really bothered him and he questioned the Lord about it.

"Lord, You said that once I decided to follow You, You'd walk with me all the way. But I have noticed that during the most troublesome times in my life, there is only one set of footprints. I don't understand why when I needed You most You would leave me."

The Lord replied, "My precious, precious child, I love you and I would never leave you. During your times of trial and suffering, When you see only one set of footprints, it was then that I carried you."

The accident didn't stop me from praying, **"Please end my life."** Finally, at the age of thirteen, I received an answer that caused me to stop praying for death. The answer came from a sweet elderly man in our neighborhood. He had a '55 Honda scooter that he rode to his part-time job. After he came home, the man offered the kids in the neighborhood his scooter to ride. I took it a couple of times and loved the feeling of freedom.

One day, one of my girlfriends and I decided we wanted to go visit a friend that lived quite a few miles away. I had a short window of being home alone and I was supposed to stay there. So we decided to borrow the man's scooter so we could see her in my short window of freedom. I wanted to be home when the family returned.

To get to our friend's home, we had to cross a four-lane highway with no lights. I was letting my friend drive the scooter, since she hadn't done it before. We arrived to see the lanes busy. With a break in the traffic, she hesitantly attempted to cross the highway. The speed limit was fifty miles an hour and she was going slower than the speed limit.

For some reason, the scooter's engine died in the middle of the intersection, right in front of the left-hand turning lane. We had two more lanes to cross. Since I had more experience with the bike, we traded places. Somewhere in the transfer, the gas happened to be turned up full throttle. When I jumped on the starter peddle, the bike's engine revved up. With it being at top speed, the bike leaped up on its back wheel, throwing my friend off the bike. I turned down the throttle, hoping it would bring the front tire back down to the pavement.

While this was happening, I saw a yellow truck in the outside lane in my peripheral sight. With my front tire hitting the pavement, I saw the yellow truck was going to be in my path and we were going to collide. Joy filled my heart as I said, "He's going to give me my wish. There is no way out of this. I'm going to die."

Instantly, my vision of the truck became a fuzzy blur, along with the screeching sounds of brakes and rubber burning on the pavement. Suddenly, everything moved in slow motion. When I reached the last lane, it surprised me to not feel the collision of the truck. Looking to my right, I saw the radiator of the truck. Today, I can still see the bugs stuck in it. Like a dream, it was moving away from me.

The next moment, I remember the bike's engine was off, as was the truck's, and we were on the shoulder of the road. Silence filled the air as I looked at the truck driver's face. His face was white as we stared at each other. Seeing my friend running across the two lanes distracted my gaze from the driver. It was then when I saw what really happened.

Every place my friend and I crossed, you see and smell the burned rubber of the truck. Yet, the tire marks were about thirty feet in front of the stalled truck. **How did the tire marks get in front of the truck?** Now, I understood why the truck looked like it was moving away. It was going backwards. I've often wondered what the driver of the truck thought about the miracle. For me, I found it hard to believe.

The truck brought me back to reality as the driver tried to start the engine, but it choked. After a couple of attempts, the engine started and he left. My friend and I decided to go home now. We were both shaken up.

When I arrived home, I found the house empty and I was grateful. The experience was daunting and I felt what happened meant more than guardian angels looking out for me. It was an answer to my prayers. I was grateful the house was empty because I needed time to think about this miracle.

Finally, I prayed and asked, Why wouldn't you let me die? I didn't hear an answer, but I knew He wanted me here and not with my mother. There was a purpose that I couldn't see right now.

I didn't feel like I had anything to give to my life. After thinking about it, I finally prayed and told Him, "There is nothing here in this life that gives me any pleasure. All my dreams are gone. I see nothing here that would make my life worth living for. I don't want to be here, but since you want me here, the only thing I can do is try. My life is yours and you can do what you want. Just let me get through it and I will stop asking you to take my life."

Something strange happened to me as I felt the responsibility of my life sliding off my shoulders. Suddenly, my burdens became lighter. In my heart, I knew He would take care of me like he did with my hand and on the road with the truck. With my heart eased, my prayers didn't stop. They just changed from me asking things for myself. Instead, I asked what I could do for others and for the first time, my broken heart eased some. It was enough for me to get out of bed and go through life where I really didn't care what would happen to me.

With me desiring to give service, even though my life hadn't changed, I found freedom and a form of peace.

Chapter 5

Teenager

By giving my life to Him, I stopped being concerned about it. My present painful moments became tolerable for me to handle. In the process of giving my life away, I didn't realize that I had embraced my circumstances. Before, I was always pushing them away, not wanting to claim my life as my own. Nothing changed in my life but my attitude and it made the complete difference. This is a very important law that we're going to talk about further in the book.

At school, I didn't have problems with friends. They were always around me. My friends weren't aware of my plight at home. I had no visible scars or any cuts, even though my father, Jen, and Don broke my heart every single day.

There was a song of the day that was very special to me and I liked the words so much that I made them a part of my life. It was called *Smile* and its message was to keep smiling even though your heart was breaking. For me, a smile was a way of giving service to others and I found that it eased my pain from moment to moment. So I tried to do it often.

Looking back, I always prayed for the right friends. If I ever felt frightened about having to deal with my home life, a friend would appear and be warm. It helped to push my home life into the back of my mind so I could get through the day. In my lifetime, I've been blessed with good friends and many.

With me starting the seventh grade, a couple of my friends and I happened to be together talking about our new school. One of the girls had a magazine called *Seventeen*. She was excited about an article regarding how to get a guy. I already had a boyfriend, I guess. Growing up, I enjoyed having boys as friends. Seldom did I ever get romantic with them. I just enjoyed having them as friends. They didn't seem to be as mean as girls can become.

The article suggested you keep a diary of everything this boy did that you want to know better. You were supposed to write down where you happened to see him and what he was wearing. The idea of keeping a diary seemed confusing to me, but the other two girls wanted to do it and I went along to be a part of the group. The one girl who brought the article wanted to know if it would work.

Quickly, I discovered I liked the diary part. Numerous times, I tried to keep a diary of my life, but it was too painful. Giving up, I decided there was nothing I would ever want to remember from my past. To my delight, I found out that I loved the writing aspects.

After two weeks, the other girls lost interest in the project. I kept going with the diary only. It gave me the opportunity to write about something non-threatening and I found something that I finally enjoyed. My diary consisted of every place I saw my "boyfriend," which was at school. So I kept track of the halls and clothes that he wore.

At school, we kept our purses inside our desks. One day, the diary happened to slip out of my purse, during my Spanish class. Not realizing it, I left it behind. The next person happened to be a ninth-grade girl that happened to be a part of the newspaper staff. Of course, she found it. Instead of giving it back to me, she printed it in the school paper without my permission. I guess you can say I was published first when I was in the seventh grade.

Instantly, everyone wanted to know who I was. This was the first time I had experienced fame. Quickly, I decided I didn't like it. Everywhere I went, people pointed at me. It made me feel very uncomfortable. Then something new happened that I never would have expected. I couldn't get down a hall without numerous people calling out, "Hi, LaRene."

Now that I look back on it, they were mostly boys and I had no idea who they were. The other group of people that surprised me was teachers. They would smile and say hello to me. This was crazy to me and I felt it was very stressful. Everywhere I went, I felt people wanting something from me. It upset me because I wasn't sure that I wanted to give or could give to them what they were looking for.

Sometimes it frightened me to have strangers walking up to talk with me. I didn't trust people to begin with and I wanted them to all stay at arms length until I knew them better. Strangers seemed to crowd me, even if there were boys involved. It bothered me so much that I wished I could've turned back the clock and made sure the diary stayed in my purse.

Fame is hard and it makes you very vulnerable to dishonest and jealous people. Shortly after it happened, I vowed **never** to allow it to happen again. The fame lasted my whole year of school.

This was the summer of the alleged accident on the bike. I enjoyed the time I did get to spend with my friends during the summer. In August, I noticed my numerous friends starting to pull away from me, except for one. When I would talk with them, my other friends acted funny and didn't seem to want to talk with me. The whole experience confused me. When school started, the last friend stopped talking with me.

I learned in high school that this one person who hung back and stayed friends with me had started a smear campaign about me. She had befriended me long enough to make sure her campaign had worked, so she could better control the situation.

This friend had decided that summer to run for student body officer the next year and figured I was her competition. Being naïve, I didn't think to confront my friends about what was going on. I just stayed quiet and took the abuse out of habit. This is how I was forced to handle it at home, so I handled it the same way with my friends.

There were other changes that year for me. At the beginning of the school year, Jen and Don decided to move. They had purchased a home that was barely under construction. It was out of the city and in the suburbs. They were going to be putting in a lot of sweat equity so they could afford the home. So it meant they would be there almost every night and on Saturdays, working on the house. After school, I had to go home and take care of their family. They had five children by now and I became their mother.

With the stress of being famous gone, I was really happier, believe it or not. The fame always put me on guard. In my mind, I just wanted to be a beautiful wallflower for the rest of my life. I wouldn't have been able to spend much time with my friends because I had to work for Jen.

Whatever my so-called friend told others, I don't know and I don't care to know. It relieved my stress from school so all I had to do was deal with my problems at home. During this time, Jen and Don stopped grounding me because they had a good excuse to have me working for them. No one would question them not being wonderful people.

When you think things can't get any worse, they do. Something happened that totally changed my physical body with scars you couldn't see. At school, we were learning how to use a trampoline in gym. One Saturday morning, Don decided to go to a local gym with friends, instead of to the house. They were waiting for something to dry. As a reward, I think, he allowed me to go with him to the gym. I wanted to practice on the trampoline with a test coming up in class.

It was February of my eighth grade. At the gym, they used a belt on me to make sure I could do my back flips. After doing numerous back flips perfectly, they took off the belt so I could do it on my own. I nailed my back flips perfectly. They told me to do one more and get off so others could use the trampoline. A bunch of young girls were waiting for their turn.

I bounced a couple of times before going for a hard jump that would give me the height for a good tuck. Going for the hard jump, my feet hit the trampoline, but my energy evaporated. Never in my life had I felt so weak. My bounce was weak and it didn't give me the height that I needed for the tuck.

For some reason, my body leaned backwards and I felt like a wet noodle. My hands didn't even go up to protect my head. I landed on my head and quickly shifted to my right shoulder with the weight of my body twisting above me. When my complete body reached the mat,

I couldn't breathe. With my body on the trampoline, I lay there, not breathing. However, I was conscious.

How long I lay there without breathing, I don't know. It seemed like forever. When my breathing finally returned, it was shallow and weak. No one touched me until I started to breathe. Then they helped me off the trampoline and had me lie down on a mat.

Then they paged for Don. I remember coming home feeling physically horrible. All he talked about was what it was like for him to walk through the women's locker room. They had to bring him through there to get to me, since I was in a special room that only women could use. Was there any mention or concern about me getting hurt? Of course not. He was excited about being escorted through the women's locker.

It didn't surprise me to have him so uncaring. He seemed detached when I almost cut off my hand from the blender. The only thing he did do for me, during the accident with my hand, was quit bothering me with his sarcastic remarks until I became well again.

After that day, I was in constant physical pain and I felt like an old woman. Now, my youth was taken even more. The middle of my back ached so much and nothing would take the pain away. I would often just sit and cry out of frustration. I complained so much about it that people around us mentioned to Jen and Don that they knew of a chiropractic doctor who might help me.

Jen finally took me to our family doctor who had stitched my hand up. He took an X-ray and shrugged his shoulders, informing us that he couldn't see anything broken and was unable to do anything for me. I cried at the doctor's office. Since she could see that I wouldn't keep quiet, Jen decided to take up their friends' offer and take me to a chiropractic doctor.

He showed her how my spine had completely turned around before he adjusted me. I found some relief from the excruciating pain with his one adjustment. The doctor told Jen that it would take numerous adjustments to get my body straightened out and he encouraged her to set another appointment. Jen wouldn't do it. Instead, she thanked him and took me home after paying him.

When we arrived, I heard them talking about what the doctor had told us. During the conversation, I heard Jen say that she didn't want to keep taking me back. My father paid her back and I saw that she hadn't changed her mind on taking me back to the doctor. So I resigned myself to live with my physical pain. From the one adjustment, I at least could stop crying.

Quickly, I forgot how it felt to be young and without physical pain. The pain never changed and the memories of how it felt to feel wonderful quickly faded. It was fifteen or seventeen years before I finally went back to a chiropractor. By then, my body was frozen in the moment of the accident. I saw numerous doctors and they couldn't get it to move. I'll explain why later in the book.

This was my body now. The right shoulder was lower than my left. My head was tilted to the left and the ribs were twisted to the right, which made it difficult to take a deep breath. My hips were messed up in every possible way. If you followed my spine down my back, you would see it was crooked. At my waist, my spine disappeared for a short distance.

My lungs were constricted, along with other things not working properly. Everything I loved to physically do became very difficult. Every sport I played became difficult for me to do. I loved to play soccer and that was out. The simplest exercises were exhausting. I looked normal and like I should be able to run. The energy wasn't there and I ached constantly.

Over my lifetime, I've heard two other people having the same accident I had on the trampoline. They did a back flip and landed the same way I did. One man was an OB/GYN in his thirties. They both became quadriplegics after missing the back flip. Every time I heard about these people, I thank my guardian angels for saving me from being a quadriplegic. It was a miracle and I've often thought about it.

In my adult year, the doctors told me I had six lumbar vertebra instead of five. I've often wondered if this extra vertebra kept me from being a quadriplegic. It's very uncommon for someone to have six lumbar vertebrae in his or her spine. At least, I've been told it isn't common and I've seen it in the X-rays.

A while after the accident, I took diving lessons. Quickly, I learned that I couldn't do a back dive properly. My body would spiral into the water, not making a complete turn. At first, my teacher became frustrated with me until he noticed my shoulder. Looking at my back, he could see my spine was crooked.

When I put my arms over my head to make a dive, my right arm was shorter than my left. Before the accident, I entered a swimming race and won. Now, my lungs hurt to even swim to the side of the pool after the dive.

After the accident, I really appreciated being alone. My energy was so drained that I didn't have the desire or strength to be a teenager. Going home every night, so I could take care of Jen's children, wore me physically out. I really appreciate single parents. It's a lot of work to bring in the money and take care of others after putting in a long day at work.

Finally, the time came to move away from the city. It happened over the Christmas holidays in the ninth grade. Yes, my friend did run for student body officer and won. Did I vote for her? I really wonder if I did. At the time, I didn't know what she had done and I probably did vote for her.

Towards the end of my high school years, I had an experience that I would like to tell you about now. One of my old friends from Salt Lake called me. It was Kathy from the group of fifteen girls that I was close to. We were all very close to each other until the one friend spread the rumors about me.

Kathy called me to ask me to forgive her. She told me what happened behind my back in the eighth grade. Somehow, the truth came out and my friends knew it was wrong to believe the lies about me. I never asked her what was said about me, since I really didn't want to know. It was easy to tell Kathy that I had forgiven her. I forgave them all before I left.

She went on to inform me that everyone in the group of fifteen paid a price for turning their backs on me. Each one of them went through the same experience that I had and knew what it felt like. The special friend who spread the rumors dropped out of school in her sophomore year. I don't know if she even graduated. The foolish girl cheated to get her dream and paid a high price for it.

I never would've run for office even if I hadn't moved. Jen and Don would've made my life worse if I was in the limelight. Every time I did something better than Jen, she would yell at me and say, "How dare you do something better than me."

My Aunt Janice did the same with people in the family. She would come up to them and say the same thing. She would inform them that she was better. I remember my cousins talking about it. They used the same words I had heard Aunt Janice use behind their backs. If Jen became upset, Don would come down harder on me with his sarcastic barrages.

Out of the fifteen girls, Kathy was the only one who came back and told me the truth. She told me about her mistake in the whole affair. They knew it was a lie and yet they participated in it. In my mind, what Kathy did by telling the truth took guts. I've thought about it and wondered what I would've done if I was in her shoes. I question if I would've had the guts to call me up and ask forgiveness. Kathy has my respect to something I wonder if I could do.

At the new place, I really didn't care what happened to me. Jen and Don went back to grounding me based upon lies so they could brag to their new friends. Since they had been there working at the house, they knew the neighbors and had made friends early.

With everything going back to the way it was, Don fully returned to being very verbally abusive. Thinking everything was going to be the same, I wasn't quite prepared for this new place. In my new neighborhood, there were a lot more boys my age. There were girls, but I didn't have as many as before.

The boys and girls in my new neighborhood were wonderful people. Everyone was kind and considerate towards each other. At my last neighborhood, there were a couple of girls older than me who were just mean. Everyone at my new school was wonderful too.

I noticed Jen and Don change too. For some reason, they changed their tactics as Jen stopped telling me what I could wear. They only would allow me to go to two parties a year with or without boys. They would deem what was a party or not. It would change to accommodate them.

The rules seemed to suit their whims. I was never allowed to even go to a campaign party to help make signs and badges for one of our friends. In our area, you didn't date until you were in high school. With dating coming up, I was told that I could only date once a month. If a boy happened to bring me home from school or a church activity and was in the car, they might consider it a date. It would depend on their moods. Again, the only time I could see my friends was at school or at a church activity. This included the girls.

I appreciated being very well accepted into my new school and it was a breath of fresh air living away from my old neighborhood. The kids seemed genuinely happier here than they did in the city.

Shortly after I started school, rumors started that the student body president and I were going together. He never really asked me. We had hardly spoken to each other and I don't remember him ever calling me. I started school in January. On Valentine's Day, he gave me a box of chocolates and a card, so I guess that made it official.

I really didn't know him, but I went along with it to stop being hit on by other guys. After living like a single parent for a year, my plans weren't to get married and have a family. I was tired of raising kids and decided it would be better to be alone than in a bad situation like what Jen was in. To find someone like my grandfather seemed like an impossible dream.

So I stuck to my plan of not getting emotionally involved with guy friends. We were friends and it wasn't going to be anything more. Kissing or holding hands was out of the question. My deep-seated reason for having this rule was the fear of having something really good happen to me. Every time it did, my life would change for the worse.

No one knew how I forced myself to always smile and be funny, so they would never find out about the nightmare I was living. In my sophomore year, I was officially voted Miss Personality. The school paper did it again in my senior year. So I wasn't an introvert.

At the end of the ninth grade, I heard through the grapevine that my boyfriend and I had broken up. This was news to me and it was okay. We had seldom spoken to each other. After spending five months with my new friends, I felt very comfortable with the quality of people who I went to school with. There wasn't the "mean girl" syndrome like I had in the city.

Since I never allowed myself to have feelings for guys, it was an easy breakup. There was one event that did upset me at the end of the ninth grade. My dearest friend, named Pameal, expressed on the last day of school, "Next year, you'll fall in love with a student body officer." When she said it, her words sent a shiver through my body. It was the words "fall in love" that terrified me. Little did I know, Pameal was predicting my future and I was so determined to stick to my rule of never allowing myself to get involved with someone.

Chapter 6

Finding Jack

A couple of weeks before school started, the Girl's Association invited our sophomore class for a tour of our new high school. I went and joined a couple of my new friends. Before the tour, the Girl's Association planned some entertainment in the cafeteria. The entertainment featured two boys and the Girl's Association president. The boys played guitars while the three sang together.

One of my friends, Brenda, leaned over and told me the names of everyone singing. She had a sister who was a senior this next year and knew everyone. With me being new to the area, I appreciated learning about everyone. Knowing the names of the boys, I decided to make sure I avoided them.

Maybe it was because Brenda mentioned one of the boys was a student body officer. Pameal's words came into my mind, causing me to feel a chill go up my spine. As I watched them perform, I wanted to make sure that I never met the student body officer and felt I could handle it quite well.

After the singing, the boys disappeared before we went on our tour of the school, which pleased me. The school was new and we were the first incoming class. After the tour, I felt comfortable that I would find my way around. Everyone seemed warm and friendly at this school and I was so grateful to get away from the city. This year, I was looking forward to school.

Soon after school started, Pameal learned that the girl at the open house dumped Jack, the student body officer. It bothered me because Pameal became very determined that we meet. If she only knew how much she had upset me by her desire to introduce Jack and me to each other. For some reason, Pameal didn't seem to hear me say, "No, I don't want to meet him."

Every time, we were all in the hallway and she saw him. She tried to get his attention, while holding onto my arm to keep me from leaving in the opposite direction. Luckily, Jack would brush her off because he was in a hurry to get somewhere important.

Like Brenda, Pameal knew Jack from her older sister. It seemed everyone in our class had a sister or brother who was a senior that year, but me. To my relief, he blew us off every time and it pleased me. I told Pameal he was arrogant and I didn't want to meet him before she tried to introduce us. My judgment of him being arrogant seemed to be right. For some reason, it pleased me to watch him brush Pameal off. It made me feel confident that I could never fall in love with him.

Jack didn't deter Pameal. Finally, she won out. A day or two later, the two of us were in a hallway alone when he came around the corner. Pameal started to say, "I have someone I want you to meet."

I started to leave as he stopped this time, but Pameal successfully stopped me. Irritated, I listened to her introduce us. He gave me a smug look and stated, "LaRene. You have a hard name to remember."

Before I could say a word, Pameal countered, "Oh, it's easy. Just remember *latrine* and leave off the T."

I shouted, "Pameal!" Ignoring me, she continued to tell him my last name would fit into the same scenario. He laughed while I wanted to melt into the floor. I couldn't believe what she just did to me. No one had ever pointed out to me that my name rhymed with latrine.

Jack immediately left, laughing. He didn't impress me and I couldn't understand why Pameal wanted us to meet. But I watched him leave, feeling relieved. By his actions, I would never talk to him again. Maybe, Pameal would give up trying to get me to meet certain guys.

Pameal and I left too. She expressed that she was pleased with the introductions. I knew she was genuine so it made it hard to be upset with her. Pameal was a person you just adored and I still do to this day. She was a very kind person. I dearly appreciated and loved her friendship.

For some reason, I didn't see Jack again in the halls. It had been weeks now and I never thought about him. One day, our speech teacher asked for volunteers from the mixed grades to help with makeup for the school musical. A different friend, named Ruth, sat across from me in the class. She leaned over and wanted me to volunteer with her. The idea frightened me when she added that this would be a good way to meet new people.

I just wanted to fit in and not be noticed. To avoid an explanation to why I didn't want to meet new people, especially boys, I agreed to join her. After school, we arrived at the room behind the stage. Along with the other students, we were sent out onto the stage to ask for volunteers. We were going to practice putting on stage makeup.

One of the students made the announcements as we watched groups of cast members meandering around on the stage. A few cast members trickled over to us. Then Jack emerged out of a crowd of people, walking towards me. I wanted to run, but I couldn't move for some reason. Arriving at my side, he said, "Do you mind putting on my makeup?"

Giving him a weak smile, I nodded. We left, heading for the makeup rooms. With him behind me, I rolled my eyes and said a little prayer to get me through this experience. As soon as we entered the room, the teacher told Jack to take off his shirt so his clothes wouldn't get ruined.

He was embarrassed and I was pleased to see it. Jack deserved it after laughing at my name. Shyly, he removed his shirt and sat down. The teacher handed me the makeup base and instructed me how to apply it. I had learned the rules on how to use stage makeup in the ninth grade in Salt Lake, but I never had the opportunity to apply what she taught us. This was a whole new experience for me.

Jack had deep-set eyes and he watched every move I made. Plus, he did something that every other boy did not do. Jack talked and he wouldn't shut up. He kept asking me questions about myself. Finally,

I asked him why and he told me that he liked to know people. This made me very uncomfortable. I would be punished if I talked about myself and I didn't want to do it.

The more I avoided his questions, the more he pushed me for answers. Years later, I asked him why he kept pushing me to talk about myself. He told me that he fell in love with my touch and he wanted to know more about me. Jack's questions were good and he would repeat them by wording them differently.

This boy was good and I had never met anyone with his skills in asking questions. I didn't want him to know me. My determination increased to never fall in love and I definitely didn't want to get married. After watching what my mother, two sisters, and brother went through, I knew it was impossible to find someone like my grandfather.

Besides, I was embarrassed with Jen and especially Don. I didn't want him to ever meet them. If I told the truth about my home life, Jen and Don would punish me.

My vague answers only seemed to heighten his interest in me. After sidestepping a lot of his questions, I finished and had the teacher come over to look at him. We took him out on the stage while we went into the audience. Jack's eyes disappeared because they were so deeply set.

She took him back, removed what I did, and finished him. What she did was right and now I understand what the other teacher was trying to teach us in class with applying the makeup.

Mrs. Bybee announced that she would have to do Jack for the play. So he was her project. I worked on a couple of more people before they let us leave. The next day, we were asked to go to the makeup room after school. When I stepped into the makeup room, Jack happened to be waiting for me. He quickly asked me to put on his makeup. I reminded him that Mrs. Bybee asked to do him. He said that he didn't mind having it done twice. I didn't understand he was so in love with my touch.

Not understanding his reason, I interpreted his words differently. I assumed he didn't want me to feel bad for not being able to get his eyes right for the stage. My wrong perception regarding him impressed me. I thought he was concerned about my feelings of embarrassment. So I put on the base makeup, leaving his eyes alone. Mrs. Bybee would finish him up.

This happened every night of the play. Since I wouldn't talk, Jack did. This time, he talked about how miserable he felt about his part in the play. He had the lead and happened to be paired off with his old girlfriend who dumped him. They had a kissing scene and he was still in love with her. He was miserable and I thought it was quite comical.

To me, they both were arrogant and deserved each other. Her attitude reminded me of Aunt Janice. She was a really good singer who had aspirations of becoming a professional. Jack was in a rock band and therefore had some celebrity status at school, besides being an officer.

The musical was good and I didn't see much of Jack in the hallways like I did when Pameal was trying to introduce us. I was relieved not to see him and hoped my encounter with him had ended. With the play over, I promised myself that I would *never* volunteer for anything again.

Jack did come back into my life. When the tickets for the November dance were printed, he invited me to the dance. I had to get my sister's permission, of course. Since it was a school-sponsored activity, they let me go. They agreed it was my date for November. Since school had started, this was my third date and for some reason it was different at home.

This time, Don insisted on opening the door for Jack and invited him in. As Jack reached out to offer his hand, Don stated, "I'm so glad to see you. Anytime you want to elope, I'll help you put up the ladder and I'll even pack her bags."

Jack was stunned and horrified. Ignoring Don, I walked past Jack and went outside to get him out of there. This would definitely be the last time I'd see Jack. He seemed upset by Don's comments. As he escorted me to the car, he stated, "He really doesn't like you and wants you out of the house."

Again, I sidestepped his comment, not wanting to talk about it. In a way, I was relieved to have Jack see how abusive Don was towards me, first-hand. If I never saw him again, I would know someone in the world knew how cruel he was. For the first time, I didn't feel so alone.

This was the only date of mine that Don exposed his cruelty to. It bothered me, since they were so concerned about their image and everything with them had to be in secrecy. Now that I look back, they didn't need me as much as they did before. Their oldest boys were getting old enough to do dishes sometimes and also baby-sit a little. It was obvious that Don wanted me out of the house. With them having a certain image with their friends, I can see the reason for me leaving had to make them look good. He had married my sister at the age of sixteen. Having me get married, he would get rid of me with them still looking good.

Surprisingly, I enjoyed my first date with Jack. He was different than anyone I had met. Most guys would talk about the weather, if they spoke much to you at all. At this age, guys would only talk to their group of friends and ignore their dates. With Jack, he talked and paid attention totally to me. He seemed to hang onto every word he could get me to say.

While we danced, Jack would hum in my ear. I thought he had a really good voice. Between the dances, he would go back to asking me questions and it frustrated him on how good I was at sidestepping them. I kept hoping Jack would give up. All it did was challenge him and I became an enigma to him. He wasn't going to walk away until he had me figured out and I didn't know this.

After the dance, Jack started to appear in the hallway again. This time, he would stop me and talk every chance he could. Jack was the only boy who ever got me to admit that I was only allowed to date once a month. When he found out that information, he asked me for the next dance weeks in advance.

It angered me that I couldn't tell him no. With him asking me so early, I never had an excuse and I wouldn't lie. The next month, I again enjoyed my time with him. After our fourth date, I became concerned. Jack wouldn't let up on asking me his questions.

He frightened me because he wasn't giving me a good excuse to dump him. Every boy I had met in the past and future seemed to have no substance compared to him. Jack was deep and very skilled in knowing how to get past my walls of protection. I couldn't let him in, so I started pushing him away. It didn't stop Jack.

Jack wanted to truly be a friend and I didn't see this one coming. Trust people? I don't think so. If I allowed him in, Jack would really hurt me, just like everyone else had. You should be able to trust your family and they used and abused me. So why would a stranger be different?

For some reason, Jack handled the situation perfectly. If he had come onto me with wanting a kiss, I would have a reason to cut off our relationship and I would have. Every time a guy would come onto me by being mushy, I cut it off, telling him that this was the reason why. Jack never gave me a kiss until he took me out on my birthday. With him asking me if he could give me a birthday kiss, I couldn't get upset and end the relationship if he had just taken it.

After our goodnights, Jack kept kissing just in front of the door. He never pushed me for more and I appreciated it. He made me feel like he really wanted to be my friend. I was concerned about him being like my family and he was getting underneath my skin. I wanted to get rid of him, but he wouldn't go.

Jack would compare me to a deer and he moved very slowly. He told me one night that he felt like if he made a mistake, I would be gone. It stunned me to hear him say something that was totally true about me. When we would go out to a movie, he would ask me if he could hold my hand. I would let him. Holding hands seemed very safe to me. During the movie, Jack would take my hand and lovingly kiss the back of it. Since he kissed my hand, I wasn't threatened and I didn't run like a deer. This was the most that he ever did and he was letting me know that he liked me very much. So I allowed him to stay.

One night, Jack made the mistake of accidentally calling me by his old girlfriend's name. I didn't say anything about it until we stopped in front of the house. This time, I leaned over and gave him a good, long passionate kiss and said, "I'm not your old girlfriend." He made me angry and I wanted to deliver the message.

I never kissed him that way again and he never repeated the mistake. He was so surprised that he didn't kiss me back and I liked it. Later in life, he mentioned that he wanted me to kiss him that way again, but I didn't. I wasn't going to get something started with him that I couldn't finish.

Soon after Jack and I started to date, Pameal started to date Jack's cousin, Sam. He was a cheerleader and a really fun guy. Jack, Sam, Pameal, and I were inseparable. We had so much fun together as friends. With Sam and Pameal always there, I forgot about my fears of Jack penetrating my walls. Our friendship went through the school year and into the summer. Even to this day, I get excited when I run into any one of them. This was the only happy time I had ever experienced in my youth and I've never been able to express it to them how much their friendship meant to me.

In the summer before my junior year, Jen and Don decided I could date once a week. I assume one of their friends told them their plan of once a month was a little too ridiculous. With Jack graduated, I didn't mind being friends with him. Sam and Pameal went different directions. In my heart, I was determined that Jack was going too. With him insisting on taking me to my high school dances, it kept other relationships from developing that I didn't want. So everyone thought we were hot and heavy.

A couple of months into my junior year, Jack made the decision to move to Australia. He left a couple of days before my seventeenth birthday. Pameal lived just down the street from me, but it wasn't the same with Jack and Sam gone from my life. Pameal and I never really went out on double dates again. So I went back to being alone because everyone thought I was with Jack.

For some reason, they didn't believe that we weren't going together. We only wrote to each other as friends and it didn't matter that Jack was in Australia. Everyone was getting caught up in their lives of being in love or out of love. I didn't fit in since I wasn't interested in the game of love. So outside of school, I didn't do much. And Don and Jen didn't ground me if I wasn't socially active.

Jack was aware first-hand of my home life, but I still couldn't talk to him about it. In my letters, I would just tell him how miserable life was for me. Jack had known a lot about Jen and Don, experiencing their lies and watching their abuse up close. So I felt safe with him as a friend.

During the summer of my senior year, I felt like I really paid for having so much fun in my sophomore year. My father finally appeared on my doorstep, wanting me to come and live with him. It would be Bud, my father, and I living together. As he took us around to find a place to live, I would listen to his words. It became very clear to me why he wanted us. He wanted me to take care of him as he would talk about me cooking and cleaning.

I was so weary of taking care of Jen's seven children now. Plus, I didn't have the physical energy like a young person should. My body still felt like an old woman's and the thought depressed me. Jen was so much like our grandmother and Aunt Janice. In her own way, she was also very much like our father. I was weary of being used by others.

Finally, I told my father that I wouldn't come and live with him. He was on his way to his car with Bud. Giving me a sharp look, he left with Bud. As they walked away, Bud responded, "I'll come and live with you."

In a huff, he headed for the car and I heard, "No. If LaRene won't come, I don't want to do it."

So I was right! If he had gone with Bud and acted more like a mature adult while taking care of my brother, then I would've joined them. With my father wanting me more than he did Bud, I was terrified of him. I had seen his anger recently and knew what he was like to live with.

There was another reason I was afraid of living with him. When I was in the ninth grade, my father became engaged to a very nice woman. He brought her to meet Jen and me. After a nice visit, I remember sitting in front of the fireplace in the living room. As she followed my father out of the door, she stopped and looked at me.

She said, "I want you to know that I love your father . . ."

Before she could say more, he grabbed her upper arm, dragging her away. They had to pass the front window and I could see the horror on her face and the expression on my father's face. He was angry and his lips were moving. So it meant he was yelling at her.

Seeing this all brought back what it was like living with him when Mother was alive. You never knew what was going to turn him into a crazy person. With the anger, what would I do if he hit me? Would anyone come to my rescue? No! At least, Jen and Don didn't physically hit me. They only did it verbally.

In anger, he called me up and told me that he was going to cut me off without any money. I responded, *"Fine."* Recently, I had just started to work at a local hospital in the kitchen. So at the age of seventeen and a senior in high school, I was totally on my own.

Being more afraid of him than I was of Don and Jen, I told him that was fine with me. When I told Jen that Dad was cutting us both off, she didn't say anything. Later, she returned and stated I could stay, but I needed to pay them for room and board. They weren't going to give me any money to support myself. The amount that they asked of me was lesser than what our father paid. But it was a tremendous amount for me, since I still had to pay for my fees at school and books. Plus, there were my clothes and any other needs I might have.

Again, they reinforced that I better not tell anyone about this arrangement. It certainly reassured me that I wasn't a part of their family. I thought about leaving and staying with one of my friends. They let me know that they would get even with me if I made them look bad in any form.

It was the hospital where I worked that I was on my own. I needed them to give me enough hours so I could pay for everything. They increased my hours to thirty a week and I was getting paid seventy-five cents an hour.

My friends never knew about what Jen and Don asked me to do. This included Jack. All Jack knew about my situation was that I was miserable. I didn't even tell him about my father, since I didn't want him to tell me to go live with him. It was embarrassing to tell Jack how badly my father behaved when a woman said she loved him.

With my body being weak, I would sleep through some classes at school and the teachers never said anything. Luckily, I did well in school so my grades weren't a problem. I give the credit for the grades and getting through my last year to the invisible arms. I spent a lot of time on my knees, pleading for the physical strength to go on for one more day and He came through for me.

With my father cutting me off, it meant that I had to pay for the doctor visits. I didn't have insurance and was just barely getting by financially. I couldn't be sick for work either. Since my accident, I had struggled to stay well. Somehow, I did and I know it was the invisible arms carrying me.

My senior year wasn't totally bleak. New doors opened up to show me that I had a talent. I didn't realize it until I was in my fifties. Soon after school started, our class president asked me to handle the senior class assembly. It was a last-minute assignment and I bawled him out when I heard we weren't having one because he had let the ball drop. So he challenged me to do it in the short window we had.

In anger, I took it on, so he handed me a book called *You're a Good Man, Charlie Brown*. It was a two-hour play and I rewrote it without hesitation so it would fit into the forty-five minutes that we had. Since I didn't have time to open up for casting for everyone, I cast it without tryouts. Since I knew the characters, I just asked the people who reminded me of Linus, Lucy, and so on.

Without thinking, I wrote, cast, directed, and technical directed the assembly. Little did I know what door I was opening up. It was a huge hit. Every teacher I passed in the halls congratulated me on it, besides my peers. The compliments from the students were nice, but the teachers' words were what I appreciated the most. They said it was the best they had ever seen.

After that day, teachers would ask me to take a subject and put it into a twenty-minute conversation segment so they could use it in class to teach. I would pop them out and never think anything about it. I thought everyone could do it. I took drama in my senior year and I performed everything in class with someone or by myself. I rewrote the segment to fit into the time allowed. My teacher never scolded me for doing it and instead complimented me.

He always liked the flow of it and how well it sounded. Most of the time, he had heard the same thing done so many times by the different students over the years. This was a treat for him, since he had taught for years.

When it came time to do the school's musical, *The King and I*, that year, they asked me to be the technical director. The teacher who usually did it had studied in New York for directing. But this year, he couldn't spend the time doing it. So he asked me. When I said yes, the teacher taught me the rules of technical directing. I took what he said and created my own style of directing.

The stage crew was all boys and they were a class. They didn't know how to take this girl appearing out of nowhere, telling them what she wanted done. They were nice about it and I appreciated it. After the musical, again, I received praise in front of the whole cast, which irritated and frightened me at the time.

If Jen had heard about it, she would've punished me for doing something better than she could do. Jen never came to the plays and I was very pleased. Mary was the only one who came to *The King and I*. She was married now and I still seldom saw her. So it pleased me to have her come to my play. My father and I weren't talking, so he didn't show up. I doubt he even knew about it.

Later in the year, the school did *Barefoot in the Park*. Again, the teachers invited me to be technical director and I did both plays at a sacrifice. I had to keep working my thirty hours a week so I could get by with money.

During the actual run of the play, I had to cut back on work. This hurt me financially, but for some reason money seemed to appear for me and I knew He was taking care of me. Out of love for Him, I paid ten percent of my earnings to our local church and I feel it was why I had the strength to go to school full-time and work the thirty hours a week.

When I directed, I instinctively knew how to do it and what needed to be done. I did it without thought and little effort. During this time of writing and directing, I discovered a love that I didn't make into a dream. Why? So far, every dream I had was taken away from me. When something nice happened, my life seemed to get worse.

Somewhere in my forties, I met my high school principal at the Governor's Mansion at a political fundraiser. He was excited to see me and wanted to know if I went professional. I was so shocked at the word **professional** that I was afraid to ask him what he meant.

He died a couple of years after I saw him that day at the Governor's Mansion. It would be nice to tell him, "Yes. I did go professional somewhere in the entertainment field and thank you for believing in me." After that day, his words never left my mind and I wondered why.

Finally, graduation came. The same night of graduation, I left for California. My oldest brother, Harold, lived there with his wife and two children. I hadn't seen very much of him since our mother's death. A couple of months before graduation, I couldn't get him out of my mind and called him for the first time in my life.

Unbeknownst to me, Bud also had requested to leave Aunt Janice's place. He asked Harold to help him by allowing him to spend his senior year in California. Harold let both of us come without having to pay him any money. I was excited to be with my two brothers and get to know them.

This was the first time I would get to know Harold's wife. To my dismay, she was a woman with bizarre beliefs. Quickly, I learned why we never saw Harold.

Tammy, his wife, made him cut all ties with his friends and family. Harold wasn't allowed to have any conversations or relationships from his past. Apparently, he had to give all of his attention to his wife.

I learned about her strange beliefs when we happened to be driving through Stockton, California. She commented that her brother lived there and I asked if we were going to stop and see him. Giving me a horrified look, she stated, "You don't have anything to do with your siblings once you're an adult. Never will I talk to him."

Inside, I wanted to hurl. She had just told me volumes about herself and I felt so sorry for Harold. Like Grandmother and Father, Tammy had a dark side. She conducted all conversations between Harold and us. This carries on to this day. If she can't be there, Tammy sets her children up to make sure we don't talk with Harold.

In the process of Tammy always talking, she exposed more of her bizarre thoughts. Tammy told me that she loved mind games with people. She learned it from a job she had. It was fun to her to act a certain way, only to manipulate the situation. It reminded me of a child having a temper tantrum in order to get their parent to do what they wanted.

Quickly, I learned Jen and Harold had married our father and I felt so sorry for the two of them. If this was what marriage was like, I knew I wouldn't live through it. I decided it would be far better to live alone than be with people who cruelly controlled your life. This wasn't something that I wanted. I had quite enough to fill two lifetimes.

It was miserable to live with her and I was so grateful it only lasted for three months. During that time, those invisible, warm arms visited me. Repeatedly, I had miracles right and left happen in those three months and I'm so grateful I went to live with Harold.

The miracles were centered on my job. My decision to come to San Francisco was based on me knowing there was a special job waiting for me in that city. Somehow, the job was important for my future. So when Tammy insisted on me looking for a job in Concord, where they lived, I went along with her, trying to figure out why she wanted me to work in Concord and not San Francisco.

I learned why after I got my job.

Tammy was upset with me going to San Francisco because it meant I might have to travel into the city with Harold. Every place I went in Concord, I was turned down so Tammy finally broke down and granted me permission to go into San Francisco, after two weeks.

In my purse, I had a list of employment agencies to see in the city. Tammy took me to the bus and I entered San Francisco for the first time alone. Not knowing my directions, I went into the wrong area of town. Not finding the street, I happened to find a police officer getting out of his car.

I went up to him and asked for directions and he couldn't believe where I was. Seeing this was my first time to the city and I was in a dangerous area, he told me to get into the front seat and he would take me to the right place.

As we came up to Market Street, he received a call and had to go in a different direction. He pointed in the right direction and I got out. Thanking him, I looked again at my list of employment agencies and found the address of the first one on my list.

When I entered the employment agency, they handed me tests to take and I immediately took them. Afterwards, I sat down to talk with a counselor. She seemed upset with my test scores and it perplexed me when she told me that she had nothing for me because of it.

The information devastated me and I was confused. It hadn't happened to me before. Eventually, I just left for the bus station.

During my time in San Francisco and especially on the bus, I felt the warm, invisible arms around me. I looked out the window, confused, trying to blink back my tears. In my heart, I knew that I needed to be in that city and there was a job there for me. I didn't know if I could do this alone.

In my prayers that night, I explained that I knew there was a job for me in the city. I went on to explain how frightened I was to go into the city without a designated place for me to go to. If the job wasn't ready for me, I pleaded for Him to allow me to sleep past 6:00 AM. If it was, then I pleaded to wake up at 6:00 AM. I promised to turn off my alarm so He could tell me when to go into the city and get my job.

I picked 6:00 AM. because with my physical condition, it was miserable for me to wake up that early in the morning. If I pushed myself too hard physically, I would get sick because my immune system was so fragile.

After my prayers, I turned off my alarm and fell asleep very quickly. The next thing I knew I was sitting up in bed. The room was dark and I couldn't see anything. So I wondered if I was still asleep and dreaming. Trying to figure out if I was dreaming or awake, I looked at my clock. It read six o'clock on the dot.

Stunned, I whispered, "I'm going to have a job at the end of the day." I thought my heart was about to burst as my chest burned, letting me know it was true. Relieved, I got up and left the house for the bus stop.

The miracle wasn't just me waking up at 6:00 AM. During the night, a picture was held in my thoughts. It consisted of a door with writing on it. The door read: White Collar Agency. Looking at my list, the employment agency was in the middle of my list of agencies. Looking at my list, I knew it was the place I was supposed to go to.

Getting off the elevator, I walked down the hall and sure enough, at the end of a hallway, I saw the same door that was in my dreams. I entered, knowing what was going to happen next. They handed me some tests and I took them. This time, I received very high scores, which was what I was used to.

This let me know that He had something to do with my test scores at the last place. He didn't want them to send me out on an interview. As I sat down with my new counselor, she opened her black book. At the top of the list, I could read US Steel. "Let's start here," she said. "This job has been open for a month and I've sent numerous people to them and they have refused to hire them." Again, I knew it was my job and He had held it open for me for a month.

It was a job working with their engineers, handling their filing. So I went to the interview and walked out with the job. US Steel had fabulous benefits and I finally had insurance and was making enough that I could support myself. It felt wonderful.

Tammy wasn't happy with my job. Usually, I rode the bus and so did Harold. Sometimes, he needed his car in the city for his job. If I rode home with him on the bus or in his car, Tammy would have an adult temper tantrum. When we entered the house, she would be on the floor of the kitchen, acting dazed.

She would act like she couldn't talk. When my brother took her into the bedroom, suddenly, she could speak very well. I could hear her threatening Harold that if he wanted to stay in the marriage, he had to obey her rules. Harold couldn't bring me home from work or ride on the bus with me. I could hear him pleading with her, but she had so much hate within her. She wouldn't bend.

Today, if I saw Harold on the street, I could easily walk past him, not realizing he was there. We know that he couldn't have anything to do with his friends from his past. I wonder if she lets him have friends in his life today.

After I left Harold's home, I heard Bud ran away from home. It had to be bad for him to run away. Bud is a wonderful, soft-spoken man. He wasn't rowdy as a child. Everyone loves Bud because he's so easy to get along with. Tammy must have gone after him with me out of the picture.

Everything isn't always black. Tammy did another strange thing that was a blessing to me. In the process of trying to get rid of me, Tammy told me that my father called and wanted me to come home. She added that he missed me. We all know it was a lie. I don't even remember my father coming to my graduation. Plus, she didn't know that he had cut all communications off with me. Since I never talked about my life, she didn't know that tidbit of information.

For some reason, I was pleased with Tammy's lie. Living with them was the same as living with my grandmother, my father, and Don.

Later, I tried to figure out how to go back to Utah, where it would be cheaper to live. Maybe, I could live on my own. So I decided to play along with Tammy.

The next day at work, I mentioned Tammy's lie to those I ate lunch with. One lady explained that with US Steel, you could get a transfer to any one of their offices. She wasn't sure about the qualifications, but she told me to go talk with the man in charge. She gave me his name as I thought about it. The idea wouldn't leave my thoughts.

The next morning, I walked into the man's office and asked him about the rules for a transfer. He told me it was based on an opening and he would check for me. He warned me not to get my hopes up. Thirty minutes later, he came to my desk and informed me that I had the transfer. I had to be in Salt Lake City on Labor Day weekend.

Obviously, I was very relieved to go back to Salt Lake City with benefits and a good-paying job. Now, I had six or seven weeks left to figure out where I was going to live in Utah. I called Jen with the news. She greeted me with coldness and didn't invite me to live with them. Their kids were old enough to take over for me now.

They did have most of my things. When I called back later regarding them, she informed me that she and Don decided I could come back, but I would have to pay them. It didn't surprise me. I thanked her, letting her think I would come. However, in my heart, I wanted to find another place.

In the neighborhood, there were three girls planning on going to Brigham Young University. I talked about moving in with them, but they were on campus and I had to be going to school to join them. In my heart, I started to pray for a roommate so I could live away from Jen and Don.

Hopefully, someone might be going to the University of Utah. They didn't have on-campus housing and I would be closer to my job. BYU was an hour's drive one way to my job. The winter roads can be bad sometimes.

With me leaving the night of graduation, I didn't know what was happening with my friends from high school. No one wrote to me, but Jack. After I got my transfer, Jack told me that he was planning on returning to the states around New Year's Eve.

With my transfer in hand, the thought of seeing Jack again frightened me. Now, I had another problem added to my list. With Jack out of the country, I had a safe friend. I didn't want anything to go any further than a friendship. Being terrified of happiness, I didn't want the crap that Mary, Jen, and Harold had to live with. They taught me that what our grandparents had was a fluke and I probably would never find it.

Before my new friends and I moved back to Utah, they invited me to a seminar put on by BYU. It took place in Oakland, California. I jumped on it, hoping that I would find someone who I could make friends with quickly so we could be roommates together.

The classes were spread over a couple of days and I enjoyed them. In the closing session, BYU had invited some singers to entertain us. During the music, I felt disappointed not to find someone to room with and I was thinking about it. I sat quietly in the dark room, listening to the music. The music happened to touch my heart in a special way.

In the quiet moment and without asking for them, I felt a warm feeling sweep over me that I would get from my invisible arms. Without thinking, I expressed, *I know you want me to get married and it's Jack . . .*

Before I could finish, I became totally consumed with a warm, burning sensation. It went from the top of my head to all the way down to my feet. I could've fried an egg from the feeling that consumed me. During that moment, I heard, "Yes. This is what I want for you."

I had been praying for a roommate. The answer to my prayers was Jack. Now, it made sense why I didn't find someone to room with. I decided to put up with the abuse at Jen's until Jack returned. The decision caused me to have peace for the first time. I trusted Him to help me get through my situation with Tammy and Don. I just hoped this same sick behavior wasn't going to continue with Jack too.

Shortly, I would be leaving California and I was going to fly for the first time. The thought frightened me, but it was my only way home. When I went to the airport, Bud and Harold came with me. Harold walked me to my seat within the plane, since it was my first time flying.

I sat down and looked back at him. It touched me to see him crying and I'll never forget it. I didn't tell him what I knew about his wife. I just hoped he cried because we would never see each other again and he loved me. This is what I wanted to believe. I loved him, even though I had zero memories of doing things with him until the last three months.

I went home to Jen's and started to plan for my future. Getting to work on the bus was very difficult, since I had no one who would take me to the bus stop. So I decided to buy my first car. Since I was alone buying the car, the salesman tried to hit on me. Sidestepping men's advances had become very easy for me. I realized all my techniques worked on everyone . . . but Jack.

When Jack returned home, it wasn't all glitter and stars. He was excited to get back into school at the University of Utah and start up his life in the states. Marriage was the furthest thought from his mind.

I met him at the airport and he explained, "I really don't want to date just you like I used to. I want to date different girls, plus you. So please don't be offended."

I nodded and countered, "That's fine. You date other girls, but don't come back to me. I'm not going to wait around and I'll be gone. We need to sever our relationship now so I can move on with my life."

Out of respect for our friendship, he asked me out and I accepted. One of the advantages of paying full price for my room and board with Jen was I didn't have to work or get permission to go out with Jack. Secretly, I believed they wanted me to get married so they could get rid of me with dignity.

Little did I know what angst Jack felt by me requesting we sever our relationship. As we got reacquainted, Jack wanted to get away from me because of Jen and Don. He told me later that he didn't want to marry me because of them. He had seen what they were like first-hand and didn't want the baggage I carried into a marriage with my family. Frankly, I don't blame him. Jen and Don were embarrassing and he hadn't met Harold and Tammy.

After our first date, Jack wanted to cut it off with me, but instead he asked me out again. For some reason, Jack became upset every time he tried to cut everything off with me. He couldn't do it. Somehow, it felt very painful for him to never see me again.

He fought with his feelings for five weeks. Finally, at the end of the fifth week, I was dropping him off from a date. Before he got out of the car, he expressed, "I think I want to marry you." Jack hoped it would relieve some of the stress within him.

After a pause, I countered, "When?"

We both sat there in silence for what seemed like a very long time. Finally, without thinking, he found himself going through the motions, not understanding why. He started talking about when we could do it.

He suggested we tell our parents first. So we walked into the house and found Jack's mother. She was very cold and his father didn't say anything. Out of respect, we tried to tell my father, but he wouldn't open the door. So I told him through the door and left. A week later, Jack surprised me with a diamond and we told everyone.

Now, Jack's life started to fall apart. He really didn't want to get married and now he was officially engaged. Panic filled his heart and he wasn't sure what to do. For the first time in his life, Jack prayed from the very depths of his heart, asking if he should go through with the marriage. After two weeks of constantly praying, Jack got the same answer I did. When he told me about his powerful answer, I expressed to him my experience for the first time and we compared notes.

Knowing he had the same experience gave me peace that it was right. We worked on the wedding for the next five months. In the beginning, my father refused to pay for it. My mother's twin sister came to my rescue. She was upset with his attitude and challenged him to take responsibility for his family. So he came and offered to pay for the wedding.

Everything for the wedding was on my shoulders. Jack helped make some decisions. For some reason, Jen refused to help me and was cold. Then she realized some of her friends would be invited to the reception. So she came back and informed me that she wouldn't help me, but she would be a part of the wedding line and I had nothing to say about it. At that point, I hadn't even thought about the wedding line and who was going to be in it.

Since I raised her kids, Jack and I invited them to serve at the reception. Jen wanted to make her kids matching vests. She informed me that was all she would do to help me with. At the time, I was taking a night class from a local business college. Knowing I didn't have a mother, my teacher offered to help me with my wedding plans.

I really wanted her help, but refused. She would have to meet my father and I was embarrassed with what might come out of his mouth. I knew if she got involved, Jen would get involved too, putting on a show so the woman would praise her on being such a wonderful person. It embarrassed me to see her put on her show. So I refused her help.

By the time everyone handed me their list of guests, I had about six hundred invites. With my mother's twin sister making sure my father came through, he didn't say anything. I think my mother was influencing her because they were very close. It was only time my aunt got involved with my life. I'm very grateful she came to my rescue.

Tammy called to tell me that she and Harold weren't coming to the wedding. The excuse was very flimsy and she was very hurtful with her words towards me. Tammy used anger and coldness in her message. There was no excitement in her voice and she didn't even ask how I met Jack or anything about him.

I took it that she wasn't going to allow Harold to be around his family. If they did come, he wasn't allowed to talk with Jen or me anyway. Mary called to tell me that she wasn't coming. She had moved to Tennessee and couldn't afford to come. The wedding took place in June so Bud could come.

A week before we married, I panicked and wanted to call it off. I didn't want to end up like Jen, my mother, Harold, and Mary. I didn't know at the time what she was going through. Jack reminded me about our answers and I felt those warm arms around me as he spoke. Trusting them, I went through with the marriage and Jack saved my life. I'll always be indebted to him. He was my first dream come true. I married my grandfather.

Chapter 7

Dying

Before we were married, the state required a blood test from a doctor. What they were testing for, I don't remember. When I went into see the family doctor, he gave me a physical examination, along with the blood test. When he finished, the doctor told me that I wouldn't be able to have any children. While he told me this, I felt those invisible arms and, for some reason, didn't pay any attention to his words.

My uterus wasn't in a position for me to conceive. Now that I look back on it, the trampoline accident had realigned everything internally right down to my uterus. Right after I received the news that I couldn't conceive, the area around my uterus cramped for days. Being in so much pain anyway, I dismissed it to the change in my lifestyle. For some reason, the cramping stayed for a month. Two months after seeing the doctor, I returned and stated, "I think I'm pregnant."

He rolled his eyes and said he would check me. The doctor was stunned to see my uterus had literally moved into the correct position, allowing me to get pregnant. So he gave me a blood test and sure enough, I was pregnant.

Our excitement quickly changed because I became very ill. I couldn't keep anything down but canned pears and cereal. It was hard for me to work, but I did. In my sixth month, I took a leave of absence from work because I could do it and still keep my benefits.

When I got married, I weighed a hundred and fifteen pounds. Being pregnant, I never gained over a hundred and twenty. With my spine twisted and everything out of place, I was miserable being pregnant. So far, everything about my life was a repeated miracle. When I turned my life over, I only asked for Him to take care of me and He was doing it.

If I felt tired before being pregnant, the pregnancy only increased my fatigue. It caused me to constantly pray in my heart to make it one more hour with some kind of physical strength and endurance. More than once a day, I felt those invisible arms around me. Afterwards, I would feel a little stronger and more tolerant of my discomfort.

When it came time to deliver, my water broke at four in the morning. Epidurals were on the scene and I wouldn't let them give me one. When I read the disclaimer, warning that if the epidural misses your spine, it could cause paralysis, I wouldn't let them give it to me. My spine was so twisted that I felt the chances were in the favor of paralysis.

Years later, I went to doctors who specialized in sports injuries. Since my spine disappeared at my waist and I weighed only ninety-eight pounds, when I wasn't pregnant, the doctor found my spine behind my belly button. You can adjust the spine through the stomach and he was wondering if it would work on me when he found it.

So you can see how messed up my body was and now I was going to deliver a baby. With every contraction, I threw up stomach juices. My whole body was in such a mess that it was struggling to perform its job.

Twenty-four hours later, the baby started into the birthing canal. If my OB/GYN had known how twisted my spine had been, he might've done a C-section. It took my son four hours to get through the birthing canal. So everyone became excited to see the baby's head finally reach the opening. Now, they were telling me to push as I was still throwing up with each contraction.

Shaking my head, I announced, "I can't push. I'm too tired."

Jack said my eyes rolled back while my lips turned blue. Then my body started to shake. They kicked him out, leaving him to pace in front of the closed doors. At the same moment, Jack's family called to see if we had the baby. Instead, he delivered the message that I might be dead. Jack's family knelt down in prayer and pleaded that the baby and I would live.

Twenty minutes later, someone opened the doors to inform Jack that I was stabilized, but unconscious. They had pulled the baby out, but he wasn't breathing on his own. A doctor for the baby entered the room while Jack waited to see if his son was going to live.

It took them forty minutes to get our son to breathe on his own. The specialist finally gave him mouth-to-mouth resuscitation before he took off on his own. Jack attributes the miracle to the prayers and I think he's right. They had always been a part of my life and I was grateful Jack was open to using prayer to find answers and comfort on a regular basis.

Two days later, I woke up to see Jack and my new son. Everything felt so strange to me, waking up. I've had surgery before and I had been purposely knocked out for three days. However, this feeling was completely different. I knew I had been somewhere else and I was trying to remember.

My memory was very foggy and I was pleased not to remember. I had so many more challenges ahead of me. It would've distracted me to remember, like I'm sure it would others who have died and returned. If someone ever talked about their near-death experiences, I can describe it right along with them. On my own, I don't remember. It seemed strange to be back and I wasn't sure if I was pleased with it until they handed me my son.

Looking into my son's face, I could see why I chose to come back. I didn't want him to go through what I did. Even with Jack being a far different man than my father, I was the only one who could stop the abuse from repeating and it was burned in my heart.

They never seemed to let me have my son for too long. I struggled to stay awake because I had lost a lot of blood. They kept me in the hospital for seven days longer to make sure I was strong enough to take care of the baby and myself.

The whole medical bill was picked up by my insurance. It cost us three times the normal delivery and we were so grateful. We didn't have the money saved up and it would've financially devastated us.

I was so grateful for His help in getting my job with US Steel. I learned after I transferred that I would've never gotten the job in Salt Lake if I stayed there. The office was small and they seldom had openings. When they did hire, they hired people who were acquaintances of those who worked there.

The person I replaced came back two months later, hoping her job was still open. She had quit and really didn't know why. The girl happened to be the daughter of someone higher up in the company. They had to turn her away. In my mind, I think I know why she left and I was grateful.

For both Jack and I, our first year was hard, but we did it together. So we were looking forward to our second year, hoping we could start enjoying our life together. Our son meant so much to us and I was a stay-at-home mother. The three of us had paid a high price to be together. Hoping the worst was over with, we moved forward.

When our son, Malcolm, turned seven months old, he received his first cold. A friend loaned me a hot vaporizer for him and we set it up on top of a five-drawer dresser close to his bed. After a couple of days, he felt a lot better. It was Sunday, so Jack was home with us.

Jack was cooking as I started to get Malcolm ready for a bath. The phone rang and someone wanted to speak with me. I had Malcolm's terrycloth sleeper down to his waist. So I placed him in his walker while I went into the kitchen to talk on the phone.

Malcolm was in a terrycloth sleeper because it was January and cold. Moments later, Jack and I heard Malcolm screaming, after a loud thud. We ran to the bedroom to see he had reached up and barely grabbed a hold of the cord that went to the hot vaporizer. Malcolm had pulled it on top of him and the water was hot.

Jack grabbed him while I ran to the bath to turn on the cold water. Minutes after we put him in the tub, Malcolm's skin started to peel off like he was a tomato. I ran back into the kitchen to call our family doctor who instructed us to get to the nearest hospital. There was a small one about five minutes away.

Jack kept him in the cold water while I found something to keep him warm. When Jack brought him out of the water, he placed him on a towel. I sprayed a burn medicine with benzene to kill the pain. I don't know if it helped, but he stopped crying and it eased my heart.

At the hospital, they took him away from us, plugging him into a tub of ice. We could only watch from a small window while we listened to his screams. They cut through our hearts.

Somewhere in the thirty minutes of this ordeal, my father heard about the accident and arrived at the hospital. He was the only grandparent or family member who ever showed up for any of our ordeals with Malcolm.

To this day, Malcolm can remember the thirty minutes in the tub of ice. He said my mother was there with him and I believe him. Malcolm explained that she told him about her experience of being burned. There was no way he would've known about it, except from her. Mamma was burned with third-degree burns before I was born. It was something that he knew more about than I did.

After the thirty minutes, the nurses had him in a crib and wrapped from head to toe in bandages. The only place Malcolm wasn't burned was the area of his diaper. It protected him, but he had third-degree burns on his legs where the terrycloth sleeper was worn. We left late that night with Malcolm in intensive care.

In the morning, they told us he had a very hard night. Around five that morning, they started to lose him. They had made the decision to call us. However, before they could make the call, his vital signs started to climb. He was burned over eighty-five percent of his body.

As they told me about his night, I could feel the warm, invisible arms around me, telling me that Malcolm wouldn't be taken from me. He knew that taking my children away from me would've pushed my ability to endure too far to live.

Knowing my son would live, I started to plead in my prayers to not let him scar much from the burns. I'd had seen others who were burned severely and you had a hard time getting past the red skin to see them. And He answered my pleas. Malcolm never needed plastic surgery like my mother and his scars are flesh-colored, instead of a bright red.

After a week in the hospital, they sent us home, since we didn't have insurance. Today, they would've kept him in the hospital and taken everything we owned to pay the bill. When Malcolm was burned, we seldom heard of lawyers suing doctors and hospitals.

For us it was very hard to bring him home. On the other hand, it was a blessing. With having Malcolm home, we had to remove the bandages twice a day. Then Jack took tweezers and removed anything growing on his third-degree burn area. Afterwards, Jack rinsed his open wounds with mineral water before applying a white paste. The area of the third-degree burn consisted of his legs and feet.

When Jack did this, our son would scream. I would sob as I tried to help. It upset Jack to have us both crying, so he would send me out of the house. The man is a tower of strength and I admired him. After spending time outside walking, I would return to find Jack putting the cream over his burn with an applicator. His cheeks were always wet from his own tears. Jack did such a good job. Malcolm didn't receive any infections, which in itself was a miracle.

The doctor said you seldom have third-degree burns without infection. In my heart, it might have been a blessing that they sent us home with Malcolm. Infections are a regular problem inside of hospitals. Without Malcolm receiving an infection, he doesn't have red scars on his legs.

Again, my prayers had been answered. We had seen another miracle. The doctor told us he wouldn't be able to tan on his legs. For some reason, Malcolm's legs match the same color as the rest of his body. They do get tanned. He didn't know any difference until he had gym in the seventh grade.

The boys made fun of his legs because you can barely see where the skin had grown together. With his legs not red, they thought he had funny skin. So he started to think he was ugly. I had seen burns and his were wonderful and beautiful. Malcolm didn't have anything to compare his scars against, so he didn't know how good his looked compared to others.

Malcolm's whole experience was a miracle. Later, the nurses said that his chances of living through the thirty minutes in the ice water were slim. Twice in his first year, Malcolm should've died. Like his mother, he was kept here. Today, he's a successful financial planner with a wonderful family.

I have a testimony that life has a plan for us, if we'll follow the guidance that is there. In my case, I knew nothing else but the invisible arms, guiding my path. Malcolm wasn't our only child who has memories of my mother being there for them. They adore my mother and they always speak of her love for them. Mamma had a way of letting you know that she loved you. I'm pleased they know her as well or better than I do.

Another miracle happened during the time of Malcolm being burned. I got pregnant again.

We were using something to prevent us from getting pregnant, but it happened anyway. With the stress we were under with Malcolm, it would've been possible we weren't using anything. However, in the future, I became pregnant with using something that was ninety-nine percent effective.

Looking back on this second pregnancy, I can see why He caused me to become pregnant. After my near-death delivering Malcolm, and him almost dying on me twice, I would've **never** become pregnant by choice. When I went to see my OB/GYN, he would just shake his head and say, "You defy everything that's in the books. You seem to write your own."

Since Malcolm had blazed the trail through my twisted hips, this delivery with our second son was smooth and quick. On my third pregnancy, I had problems again. For the first time, I tried to get pregnant. My body was too worn out from not functioning properly in its everyday duties. I shouldn't have been pregnant.

This time, I wasn't sick and throwing up. Instead, I couldn't stay awake. Sleep would take over anywhere and everywhere. For me to fall asleep sitting up was a miracle with my twisted body. Normally, it takes me about twenty to thirty minutes to even fall asleep at night, when I lie down.

Each day, my inability to stay awake increased. In my heart, I knew I was dying. I could feel my body shutting down. It was the same feeling I had delivering Malcolm, but it seemed to be going in slow motion. This time it didn't please me. I pleaded for Him to allow my baby to live. He already knew He could take me anytime He desired. So I spent a lot of time praying for my baby to live.

Everyone around me noticed this pregnancy was different. My skin was gray and we already discussed I was too thin. Ninety-eight pounds doesn't look very attractive. I never put on weight until I completely stopped having and chasing children.

I was about four months pregnant when I happened to hear about a medical doctor lecturing in Salt Lake. He was talking about preventive medicine. It was a new concept in the seventies. The doctor happened to be from California and I had a strong feeling to go hear his lecture. I knew by going there, I would receive a strong answer to my prayers regarding my baby's life.

With my back being so twisted, I seldom could stand to sit for very long, especially during a pregnancy. So I walked in the back of the auditorium and listened. After his lecture, he left while someone else spoke. When he left, he happened to pass me. He stopped to stare at me before leaving. With that moment, we connected and I knew if my baby was going to live, I needed to go see him. Yet, what he talked about had nothing to do with my condition.

My whole body burned with the confirmation that my thoughts were correct. I told Jack about him when I returned home and he received the same burning sensation. So we started to plan on how we would get down to California. We didn't have a lot of money and to see this doctor would probably take everything we had in savings. Insurance wouldn't cover him, because he was involved in the new practice of preventive medicine.

When we told Jack's family and some friends, they became upset and told us we were crazy. Every time they tried to stop us, peace consumed us when we thought about going. In our hearts, Jack and I knew that I was dying and we couldn't explain it to others. Against everyone's advice, we set the appointment and left.

When the doctor heard I was pregnant, he refused to see me. His staff pleaded with him to change his mind, using the excuse of the long distance we traveled to get there. Eventually, he agreed. With his staff on my side, they started me through some tests. I deeply appreciated these tests. For the first time, I could see how poorly my body was functioning. X-rays didn't cut it.

They started off with a heat sensory that would read the different temperatures throughout my body. The doctor had the theory that our arteries can become easily blocked. He had medicine that would clean out your arteries so the proper amount of blood would reach the right areas. It was supposed to stop you from developing diseases caused by your body being improperly nourished.

After the blood test, they took pictures of my body heat in black and white, besides color. They both were striking and compelling for me to see. The black and white pictures were taken from the neck up. If the pictures showed white, then it meant the areas were getting a good source of blood. If it was black, then it meant my body was getting less than twenty percent of my blood supply.

It didn't surprise me to see the right side of my neck black, meaning I was receiving inadequate blood flow. The right side of my head was where I hit the mat of the trampoline, forcing my right shoulder to take the brunt of the fall. The only white area in the picture was the left side of my neck. My face was completely black.

Now, I understood why I always had a dull headache and always felt light-headed. I also couldn't blush and it made sense. There wasn't enough blood flow to allow me to blush.

When they took the color picture of the heat in my back, I was really taken back. They were shocked too. If you had a good source of blood, the color was red. The color blue meant you were receiving very little blood in that area. Nothing in my back was correct. Where I was supposed to have red, the color of blue was there. They were shocked and had never seen anything like it before. For the first time, I could see underneath the skin what the chiropractor had explained to Jen and me.

After the test, the staff sent me to the physical therapy room. They had me lie down on a machine to place my head in a harness while putting straps on my ankles. The harness upset me as it forced my head in a position that was very uncomfortable.

Looking up at Jack, I asked him if my head looked straight. He had a very good eye for what looked straight and he thought it looked great. They turned on the machine and slowly it stretched my neck and feet in opposite directions, while steel balls moved up and down my back.

After the second day, I happened to turn my head and it suddenly shifted on the axis from my left to my right side. It felt wonderful. I could feel new blood pumping into my head. Since Jen never took me back to the chiropractor, certain vessels were being blocked from getting blood to my head.

At the end of the week, they repeated the black and white pictures of my head and neck. The right side of my neck was white like the left. You could start to see the outline of my nose, eyes, and lips. The medical doctor couldn't believe it when he saw it. For the first time, he wanted to talk with me. He wanted to know how this was possible when he gave no medicine that would clean out my arteries. So I explained to him about the accident and stated, "Wouldn't it be possible that blood vessels get pinched or nerves are blocked so they can't deliver the message properly on what I need?"

This was a totally new concept for a medical doctor in those days. They thought everyone needed to be cured with a pill. To me, I never could understand why it was so new. It's just common sense. If the nerves and blood vessels become blocked, why should they work properly?

Before I left, the doctor did two things that saved my baby's life. He put me in an oxygen chamber every day. Oxygen was being pumped into every cell of my body and it felt wonderful. My poor deprived body needed it. The picture showed that I wasn't getting enough oxygen to my head especially.

They also fed me intravenously with vitamins and nutrients for the baby. With my digestive system in such bad shape from the trampoline accident, this was wonderful for me. Every day for a week, they did all three things. When I arrived home, people couldn't believe the difference in how I looked. My skin was pink and I had more energy since the trampoline accident. It wasn't perfect, but I had improved and it gave me hope that I could find a way to unwind all of my scars and reach good health.

We delivered a baby girl who did show signs of lack of nutrition during her time in the womb. Some of her baby teeth didn't develop enamel on them. She also struggled being able to hear her vowel sounds. Some people believe it has to do with the nutrient problems in the womb.

Anyway, my prayers were answered. She lived and was a very happy baby. I deeply appreciate her being in my life. I'm grateful we both get to go on with this life together.

Chapter 8
I Found Me

As our children got older, we had challenges just like every other parent. Our second son, Josh, was a very grumpy baby. With age, he seemed to become worse. For some reason, he had a huge chip on his shoulder, which caused him to become angry without notice. We were constantly pulling Josh off of other kids with him using his fists on them.

This was his way of communicating his displeasure. He didn't seem to respond to anything we said to him and the habit continued. As Josh turned four, he didn't improve and I was afraid for myself. I pictured him towering over me as a teenager, being angry. He would hit first and ask questions later. Everything we tried with Josh didn't seem to curb his temper.

In desperation, Jack and I focused on him in our nightly prayers together. We pleaded for a way to reach him. After two weeks of praying, Jack came up with an idea. It opened a door for us with Josh. Looking back, Jack was the only person who would've accepted the answer from our prayers. My fear wouldn't allow me to hear the answer.

The idea that came to Jack seemed very strange and unproductive to me. He felt that we needed to teach Josh how to love himself and he would stop being angry. Curious to learn how Jack was going to accomplish this feat, I followed him and Josh into our main bathroom. They stopped in front of a six by four-foot mirror and Jack made Josh face himself. Then he instructed Josh to say, "I love Josh."

He fought Jack, but his father wouldn't back down. It made me feel uncomfortable and I wanted to stop Jack. For some reason, I couldn't open my mouth to protest. So I left to hear Josh finally mumble out something. Jack gave him a goal of saying it to himself in front of the mirror twenty-five times. I rolled my eyes and avoided them.

In my amazement, Josh started to change. He became happier. One day, Jack invited me in to see Josh repeat his words, *I love Josh,* twenty-five times. Grinning, Josh passed by as Jack smiled at me. Reaching a hand out to me, he asked, "Can you do it?"

Fear consumed me as I attempted to follow Josh. I said, "Sure, anyone can do that. It's easy." Before I could leave the doorway, Jack had a hold of my wrists and yanked me into the room. Leaving me in front of the mirror, he stood in the doorway and said, "You do it."

As I stared at myself, I became even more afraid. The fear became so strong that I felt like Jack had just shoved me into a cage with a hungry tiger. I felt trapped, fear charging throughout every cell of my body. I looked at Jack with my face as white as a ghost. Not giving him notice, I charged him, expecting him to move.

He didn't and I was so afraid. Not realizing what I was doing, I stepped on his thigh, attempting to climb over him. Jack grabbed a hold and pulled me down. With his arms wrapped around me, he easily brought me back in front of the mirror and repeated his words.

Seeing myself in the mirror, I fought to get away from his grip. Being only ninety-eight pounds, it was easy for Jack to hold me. He repeated his words and I pleaded with him to let me go. When he said no, I felt the invisible arms join him.

Being so familiar with Him, I pleaded with Him to help me get away from Jack. Instantly, I knew He was on Jack's side as well. Looking at myself, I started to cry from the depths of my soul. By doing it, I saw in my mind all of the layers of shock that I had endured at the hands of others. For the first time, my soul felt the love from the invisible arms.

After being in Jack's and my creator's arms, I couldn't get the vision of all the layers of scars out of my mind. What were they made from?

How could I see them now for the first time? I had so many questions, not realizing what was being opened up to me. Hope was being breathed into my life, my soul, and my heart for the first time. It was a chance to rid myself of the pain I had endured for so many years. It started to consume me.

Jack saved my life that day. Innocently, he and the invisible arms had taught me a very valuable lesson. Our spirit can die without **love**. The vision taught me that we do carry invisible wounds inside of us. They are very powerful and crippling. The scars will stop us cold in our tracks from enjoying life. And we can't **will** ourselves to move past them. I tried with the interviews and it didn't work. It was a testimony to me of how well Jen and Don had created **fear** within me, so I wouldn't ever talk about them.

So how do we handle wounds that live inside of us?

This was my burning question. With no manual on how to heal my wounds, I wondered what I would do. So far, I hadn't figured it out. In frustration, I had turned my back on them, hoping they would melt away in time. Now, the whole idea of how to heal became daunting to me. But the dream wouldn't go away. Each day, my dream became stronger.

I knew I had found myself and I had seen first-hand how scarred I had become. The whole moment reminded me of the story about Dorian Grey, who always looked wonderful because his sins were kept on a picture of himself that stayed in an attic. I knew my mind, spirit, emotions, and body were scarred deeply at the hands of others. The knowledge wouldn't let me rest. I had to help myself now that I had found me.

After this experience, my prayers started to change in a positive way. I prayed for guidance to find a way to help myself. Little did I know that it would take me on a path that is difficult to describe. My heart gravitated towards positive-thinking books and I loved them.

The first book I read was called *The Magic of Thinking Big* by David J. Schwartz. Then I moved to *Think and Grow Rich* by Napoleon Hill and *The Power of Positive Thinking* by Norman Vincent Peale. My list kept growing. I started to see a pattern of a few principles being the same.

So I wrote them down, determined to understand why I was seeing the same principles in all the books.

I wanted to understand why you needed to visualize before realizing what you wanted to happen in your life. Why do you need to think positively about your future? Won't it just come to you in any way it wants? I had questions about these new concepts. When I asked why in my prayers, my dream to be healed grew more, leaving me to search for the answers. Every time I tried to visualize happy moments in the future, it hurt deeply. Looking into the future reminded me how my dreams to be a part of a family never came and it never would.

Something so simple became the hardest thing for me to do. In a way, it angered me to have it be so hard. I felt it was hard because the scars were so thick and severe. It was difficult not to blame others for my trials. Deep down, I did blame them. Through my struggle, my desires only kept growing.

As I continued to read and ponder on how hard it was for me to look at my future, a man from my past kept coming to my mind. I only met him briefly. I was fourteen when he crossed my path. He looked at me and stated, "Love your trials. They are who you are."

I smiled and walked away. When I was by myself, I started to scream, "How dare he ask me to love my trials. He doesn't know what I've been through." Somehow, I felt he did know and his words haunted me. In anger, I kept pushing them away, causing them to stay just outside of my attention.

Now, I found his words coming back, along with the anger. So I decided to let go of my anger and try to understand why his advice seemed to be so haunting. When my anger left me, I saw the vision again of my many layers of scars. In my mind, I reached out to them and started to say, "I embrace you. You are a part of me. So how do we heal?"

The outpouring of my love towards the layers of scars started to ease my pain to look into my future. I could only peer into the future for a moment. At least, I was starting to do it. It gave me hope to keep going forward so I could find the answers on how to heal my mind, emotions, spirit, and body. My body still hurt very much from the trampoline accident.

With a prayer in my heart, I moved forward. Every time I thought about quitting, the vision of my spirit being touched by my creator gave me the courage to keep going. For me, I was in so much pain and it felt so heavy on my heart. I desired the soothing peace that I felt in the vision. In my heart, I saw it as my reward to finding a way out from the darkness that seemed to consume my future and past. Stepping forward, I was determined to find peace for all four areas of me.

Looking into my future wasn't the only issue I was learning from books and tapes. There were more and I will talk about them in the next chapters. I'll tell you how I felt and what I learned. I did find the answers to my burning questions and found the peace I saw in the vision.

Join me.

Chapter 9
Looking at a White Piece of Paper

Why would I start a chapter with "White Piece of Paper"? During my research, I found themes that seemed to be in multiple books. One caused me a lot of problems that took me years to unravel. It was: you can start a new day with a white piece of paper. On it, you can write anything that you want. You can become anything you want.

They were talking about positive affirmation. I wanted to change my feelings and feel wonderful. This concept made sense to me. Every book had this method. You repeat positive statements out loud that you want to have happen in your life. Then the things you ask for will appear.

Someone recommended to me Og Mandino's book, *The Greatest Salesman in the World*. I enjoyed my first page. The first couple of chapters are about a man seeking the greatest salesman. When he finds him, the salesman divulges his secrets to the protagonist. His secrets were a page and a half long.

The salesman promised his advice would change the protagonist's life if he would read one secret a month out loud, three times a day. Each month, the salesman would give him a new secret.

So I did what the greatest salesman suggested. I faithfully read one chapter a month, which took me about a year to finish the whole book. Afterwards, I went to his other book, *The Greatest Secret in the World*. At the end of eighteen months, I became discouraged. Nothing inside of me had changed.

Other people I knew were getting results from his affirmations. Why wasn't I? What made me so different? The answer to my questions came twenty years later. It came in a very strange way.

It happened to be during the holidays as my two oldest daughters came home from attending Weber State University. Malcolm had graduated from Weber State with a degree in Sales. He had mentioned numerous times for me to take one particular professor's class. He did more than just teach you about sales. Malcolm felt his classes gave you the tools to use in your day-to-day working relationships.

After listening to Malcolm talk about it, I promised myself that I would someday take his classes. Maybe, he would teach me something new. While at the dinner table, my oldest daughter asked her younger sister to take his classes with her. She went on to say that she heard he was taking a three-year sabbatical at the end of the semester.

Sighing, I mentioned that I always wanted to take his classes too. Both girls agreed to take his two classes together and invited me to join them. I agreed, not wanting to pass up an opportunity. In case the classes were boring, I would at least be with my two girls.

When I paid for the classes, a strange feeling swept over me. I felt something very important was going to happen in my life because of these classes. I felt it was going to be for the good.

In class, I paid attention to everything that was going on around me, looking for something that I felt would happen. As the semester entered the last stages, I still had this feeling that something important was going to happen to me. The closer the class was to end, the more eager I felt to go talk with the professor.

I kept telling the feeling to go away or tell me what I was supposed to say to him. The feeling did not leave me, but only increased. As the feeling felt stronger each day, I finally got tired of it. After class, I went up to the professor and asked if I could talk to him. He nodded and invited me to follow him to his office.

Other students would come up to him to talk as he made his way towards his office. I followed behind, praying the words would come to me. He entered the building and I was thinking about running away.

When he disappeared through the doors of his office, I prayed to either learn why I needed to talk with him or to be released from this powerful feeling.

When I entered the room, he was standing behind his desk. To my amazement, I heard myself say, "You have a message for me. What is it?"

As he stared at me, I wanted to melt into the floor and disappear. I ordered my feet to take me out of the room, but they wouldn't move. Slowly, a smile crept across his face as he looked down at his desk and reached out for a card. Picking it up, he handed it to me. I took it as he said, "This is my message to you. Go see this man."

I took the card and thanked him. Out in the hallway, I didn't know if I should cry or be excited. What I just did was terrifying. Exiting the building, I decided to finally read the card. Printed on it was "Thought Pattern Management." Underneath the title, I saw the name Robert Fletcher, along with his telephone number. The moment I read the card, my chest burned. It let me know that I had received the message that I was sent to find.

Thinking I would contact this Robert Fletcher sometime in the future, I placed the card in my wallet, relieved to have the feeling gone. The next week, the professor made an announcement. He wasn't going on sabbatical anymore to Brazil, so he announced that he would be teaching again at the school.

My thoughts went back to why I took his class. It was because of the sabbatical that I came to Weber State University for his classes. The news made me realize how important the card might be to my future. I thought maybe I should move on it now and learn why I needed to find this Robert.

When I went home, I called Robert W. Fletcher. His assistant set an appointment for me to visit with him. Just like the professor, I entered his office, having no idea as to why I was there or what I was going to say to him.

Sitting down, I asked, "Are you going to be teaching a class? I'm supposed to have you teach me everything you know."

He leaned back in his chair and smiled, "So you're the one I've been waiting for." Robert proceeded to tell me that he was thinking about doing it, but he wasn't sure. We parted with him promising to contact me if he wasn't going to teach a class.

In September, he started the class with two other people besides me. Quickly, I started to understand why I was there as he explained how our mind works. I spent two years with him. What I learned from Robert Fletcher cemented all the numerous things I had learned from the books and tapes. I learned why affirmation didn't do anything for me. Being with him, I understood why and how the principles in the books and tapes worked, even though the first year frustrated me.

We spent the first year talking about **words**. I thought words were the most boring subject you could ever talk about. In the past, I had little patience for them. As a little girl, I always said, "A picture is worth a thousand words. So why be bothered by them?" By the end of the year, I had a completely different opinion about words. They are extremely powerful and in my opinion very few people understand how they can control our lives.

So why are words so important to our minds?

Our words express our thought patterns. By listening to how someone places their words, I could know more about others than they were aware of themselves. I've fallen in love with words and now appreciate them.

You are probably wondering how you can learn about someone by just listening to them talk. To give you an example, I can speak and write very clear, unless someone asks me to pull information from a traumatic area. In seconds, my words can go from being clear to being jumbled into disjointed thoughts.

Why? My mind wants to protect me. When you have felt trauma, the mind stores the complete memory, including the pain and fear. So when my mind went to an area to retrieve information, it would pause for a second before it would go to another place to find the same information.

In my case, I had so many traumas from living with my family. My mind struggled to find a safe place to pull information. The mind will and can block many moments from you if they're too painful. Your mind very much wants to please and protect you.

Another problem with retrieving information from a traumatized moment is that the mind doesn't necessarily let you know the words are coming from this emotional time of your life. The tone can change to match the words from the traumatic time and the person speaking doesn't even realize it.

Now, the person listening to the words can become offended and snap back. In seconds, you could have a fight break out where no one is really at fault. The two people are reacting to each other's tone. For me, it's very hard and takes a lot of discipline not to react to people's tones when they're speaking. Since I have learned how the mind works, I try to be a lot more patient with others. We are usually harder on ourselves than we are on others.

How could trauma from our past ever affect our future?

Let me give you an example from my life. The time I spent with Robert was in the nineties. Robert showed me how to unlock my mind so it would accept affirmations. As you read further in the book, you'll see how I did it. Right now, I want to talk about how trauma can stop us from becoming who we really are.

In November 2000, I happened to be a principal real estate broker. This only means that I was licensed to supervise other realtors. For the first time in five years, I had sold my entire inventory. Since the holidays were a time people usually aren't interested in placing their homes on the market, I decided to take a well-earned break to spend time with my grandchildren and husband.

Five days in my hiatus, I started to cough and overnight I completely lost my voice. If I tried to force a whisper, it would send me into a hard coughing spell. There was nothing wrong with me, except I had no voice and my lungs struggled to take a deep breath. I had never had this problem before. The doctor said it was viral and I would have to wait it out.

Sleeping became difficult. In my sleep, I'd sometimes take a deep breath and the coughing would wake me up. We quickly found humidifiers and air purifiers that seemed to calm down my coughing, helping me breathe a little easier. If I stepped away from them, my problems would worsen. They only helped a little, but did nothing to cure my problem.

In the year of 2000, email wasn't that popular so a phone was a realtor's lifeline. With it impossible for me to use my voice, I found myself restricted to a room in the house with nothing to do. This is hard when you're used to being on the go constantly. I found myself bored and wished we were back in the Bahamas. In October, Jack and I had spent a week on the islands.

Staring at my computer, I wondered if I could write a story that would entertain me while I was sequestered in my home office. Being afraid of actually writing, I decided to explain my story through conversations of the characters, promising myself that no one would ever read it. Feeling at peace with my plan, I asked my mind to give me a story that would hold my attention until I got well.

At first nothing happened, but I waited. I didn't have any place to go. After a long moment, I heard the words in my mind. "Timeout! I hate timeout." I had no thought of where the story was going. My mind just gave me one paragraph at a time. Before long, I was spending at least eight hours a day, writing.

I was excited to wake up in the morning just to see what was going to happen next. My coughing woke me up at five in the morning, but I didn't mind. Not being a morning person, it was fun glancing out my window at the sun rising over the mountains.

My last two children were in college, so I was alone most of the time. When our married children stopped by to visit, they would ask me what I was doing. Shyly, with my voice still gone, I wrote on a pad of paper what I was up to. Malcolm stopped by each day to check on me. Seeing me writing, he started to beg to read what I was spending eight to ten hours a day writing.

After telling him no numerous times, I finally gave in because I trusted him not to laugh at me. He stopped by the next day, wanting to read more pages. He was excited to learn what was going to happen next. Each day, he stopped by after work to pick up more pages.

During the holidays, we joined together as a family. In front of his siblings, he would ask me questions about the culture and history of the people in my story. To my surprise, I could easily answer him on my pad of paper. I still had no voice and my coughing hadn't left me.

Josh wanted to read my story too and I was shocked. He never read for entertainment. Josh read for information only. He lived close to Malcolm and they started to share pages. The next day, Josh called me, upset. Since I couldn't talk, he wanted me to know that he had stayed up until 2:00 AM, reading, and had to get to work at 6:00 AM. Josh was as excited about the story as Malcolm and I were. Quickly, the other children wanted to know about the story and the kids passed the pages around.

By February, I was still sequestered in my home office. My children all loved the story and wanted me to get it published. I refused for reasons I didn't want to tell them. If I wrote the story into a novel, it meant that I would have to face the demons inside of me. Every time they saw me, the subject came up. By the end of March, they had worn me down and I agreed.

Days after I made the commitment to get my story published, my voice returned and the coughing disappeared. Not wanting to get sick again, I knew in my heart that I had better keep up my promise to my kids. What my kids didn't know was I struggled to communicate in written words or a speech.

To be honest, I was terrified to write. I prayed and asked for help to get out of my promise with dignity. Making one last-ditch effort to get off the hook with my children, I decided to send the first part of the series to a very small local publisher. They accept manuscripts as a contact. I asked them to tell me if it was worth the work to turn this story into a novel. It took them three months to answer me. They said my story was very strong, but they couldn't accept it in the condition it was in. However, they wanted to see my rewrites. Resigning to the fact my last door had closed, I chose to face my demons again.

I knew it wasn't an accident that I had been sick from November through March. In my heart, I didn't want to face my demons. At the time, I thought my biggest fear was tied to Jen. She would punish me if I out-preformed her in anything. Even though she couldn't touch me today, it meant I had to heal from the fear she had placed inside me. Little did I know that my fear of Jen was nothing compared to my other fears.

In my heart, I believe you never fail until you quit. When something blocks your path, then you need to figure out how to go over, around, under, or through what is stopping you. My story now was like a double-edged sword. I loved the time I spent with my characters. Now, I had to take my story out of screenplay format and flesh it out with all the history and traditions.

So I started to write it out and let anyone read it who asked to. Deep down, I wanted them to say, "Oh, I think I know this story. Let me write it for you." For some reason, when we feel like we're over our heads, we want someone else to bail us out. Sometimes, it's good to have them come to our rescue. Other times, it could be the worst thing that could happen to you. There are times when we just need to face our fears and see it through. This was one of those times and I struggled with it.

In my prayers, I was praying for someone to show me how to write the story. Finally, I got my wish.

Jack's nephew's wife happened to be passing through town and they were moving from Boston to Denver. She had a degree in editing and publishing and agreed to read a couple of pages. I was relieved when she told me what I was doing wrong. There are rules that you need to follow for writing a novel. They are a little different than just writing to communicate.

For some reason, I totally understood what she was saying. It all made sense to me and I became excited. So I started writing the story over. When I had someone read it back to me, I was stunned to see my words were different than my thoughts. My writing sounded like a frightened little girl.

With my training, I knew it meant that during the time of when I was learning how to communicate, something had frightened and traumatized me. I asked my mind to take me to the origin of my fear to communicate. In my mind, I could see my father's face as my mind started to play back for me what happened.

Somewhere between the age of eighteen months and two years, my father decided to help me speak better. I was happy and felt very confident about my speech. When I spoke, it was very fast. I had so much to say that I would let it rip. I think I could've made a good auctioneer.

He started out laughing at my speaking ability and that would've been fine. Then he crossed the line when he added, "She has a problem and I don't think she can ever talk properly." He went on, forcing me to repeat my words numerous times while placing my tongue at a certain place within my mouth. Today, I still have no idea what he was trying to accomplish.

This was damaging. He did this a couple times a day. Also, he would leave me, shaking his head, and say, "She's terrible. I don't think she'll ever be able to talk right." Then he would start to laugh. My father repeated this for weeks. I became afraid to speak or get caught speaking when he was around. His laughter hurt me deeply and now I understood what it meant. My father had taught me to associate fear to my ability to communicate. When you write, you are communicating.

Without the knowledge that I had obtained from Robert, I would've gone to my grave not being able to communicate so someone could understand me clearly. No matter how hard I would practice in my mind to explain something clearly, my words would make me sound like a frightened child. I couldn't control it. Would it become worse if I felt, falsely or truly, that someone was going to judge my ability?

In a later chapter, I'll explain how the mind holds onto these moments and processes information. I will also tell you how to erase these traumatic moments and heal your mind. The minute I erased the fear from Father that I had associated with writing and giving a speech, my writing and communicating skills changed instantly. I didn't even sound like the same person writing. Finally, I felt a heavy load lift off me. With my mind free, I finished my story and it was fun.

Chapter 10
I Found Love

I smile when I hear my seven-year-old grandson whining, "Life isn't fair! Why doesn't my brother have to do it too?" Oh, sweetie, life is fair if you understand the rules. The rules are what I like to dub **the laws that govern the causes and effects of what happens in our lives.**

When my mother died, everything in my life changed. Being surrounded with dysfunctional personalities, I learned a lot. I had the rare opportunity to see first-hand what my father and other siblings went through to become the kind of people they were. The opportunity I experienced to see everyone's complete true selves was priceless. I appreciate it so much because of the information I gleaned from it. It's so important to understand two questions: Who's in your life? and Why did it have to be this way?

In our last chapter, I talked about how other people's words can cripple us. In this chapter, I want to talk about something else that's just as crippling. It is **shock**. By letting you into my past, it should help you understand how shock can cripple you even more than words.

You're probably wondering, *Why are you using a whole chapter on shock? Doesn't shock melt away after the first couple of moments?* No, this is the problem with shock. It never leaves you. To give you an example, I want to talk about my father making fun of my ability to talk.

When he made me repeat my words and place my tongue in a certain spot in my mouth, he shocked me. I was shocked to hear him say that I would never be very good at speaking. Since shock always stays with you, this stopped me from being able to communicate my thoughts and feelings through writing or speech.

This stopped my ability to improve after many decades.

What stopped me? Was it my father's words or was it shock?

Shock! My father shocked me every time he pointed out to me that I couldn't speak as well as he wanted me to. I thought I was doing fine. He disrupted my ability to grow into being a good communicator. When he forced me to try to speak better, I felt both humiliated and shocked. It didn't help that I didn't understand what he was trying to get me to do.

What happens to your mind during the moment of feeling shocked?

To make this easy, we all felt shock when we heard about nine-eleven. Every person in the world felt shock when they heard about the twin towers in New York City being hit by the two airplanes. We all know exactly where we were standing when we heard about it.

If we go back to the thought of nine-eleven, our memories will bring back to us all the smells and feelings we were experiencing at the moment. You'll even remember if you were sick or not.

Since my father traumatized me, the shock froze the memories of fear, humiliation, knowledge, and pain when he said that I couldn't communicate. Now every time I had to communicate information, my mind processed any new information through the frozen image of my father belittling me.

My mind wouldn't allow me to change my ability. I will talk about why in another chapter. I want you to understand here that your mind processes new information through these frozen moments of shock. The hard part is we can't see how we are behaving. Let me give you a couple of examples.

When I tried to write, I didn't see myself in shock. My mind was processing the story through the frozen moment of my father. I couldn't hear the frightened child. Even if I read it out loud, I couldn't hear it, because my mind was processing it. My mind was scarred and

I didn't know it until I had an opportunity to stand back and see it. When someone read out loud what I had written, then I could see what other people saw.

Shock scars our minds and if our minds retrieve information from our damaged areas, we also take out anger, frustration, bitterness, or love with our information. Many times, we are offended by people's tones before we are by their words. It's our responsibility to not be quick to take offense of other people's tones.

What happens when you feel shock from an accident to the body? Is it the same as hearing someone's words?

Shock is shock. If you're in an accident, your mind, spirit, emotions, and body are all affected with shock. Let me tell you from my experience what happened to all four areas. When I had the trampoline accident, my body became frozen in my new altered state. My body refused to shift back to its proper place.

Your body stores memories within itself. When the doctors tried to move my body back into place, my body wouldn't allow it. The shock from the accident prevented it from happening. Within the memory, my emotions stored every feeling I had at the time of the accident.

It was meant for your mind, emotions, spirit, and body to work together. An accident can change this. **What happens to their ability to stay together after they have experienced shock from an accident?**

During my class with Robert, he happened to be talking about this very thing. I happened to have my legs crossed as I listened to him. Suddenly, my right foot started to jump involuntarily. It reminded me of when a doctor would hit your knee with his little rubber hammer.

Robert paused and so did my foot. When he started again, so did my foot and I was embarrassed. I quickly put both feet on the floor and it still wouldn't stop. Every time he spoke, my foot would jump to his words.

Stopping, he said, "Your body wants to be fixed. What happened to you?"

I quickly explained about the trampoline experience. Apparently, my mind, spirit, emotions, and body wanted Robert to do something. Without thought, I knew what they wanted before I consciously understood what was going on. Robert nodded and asked me to join him up front.

I sat on his chair while he stood behind me. Knowing how to program the mind, he started to speak softly to only me. He asked my mind to reattach itself to my body, emotions, and spirit. To my amazement, I could feel it happening. It was perplexing to me that shock would've caused all four areas to detach from each other. If I had gone to the chiropractor immediately after my accident, they would've stopped the shock from taking over my body and mind. The shock can hold you in a place and will not let you go unless you know how to remove it. I will talk about it later.

After the class with Robert, I thought about the moment of Robert reconnecting my mind to my body. The idea started to percolate inside of me that maybe my desire to live with a normal, healthy body could come from my mind. So I decided to try it.

I asked my mind to remove the shock from my body, allowing my body to go back into its proper place. It frightened me at first to have my mind retrieve a memory in a muscle. Memories are stored within your body in the form of chemicals. As my mind opened up each chemical, the muscle, ligament, bone, or soft tissue relived the accident. The experience taught me that every cell of my body experienced the trampoline accident.

With each chemical, I felt the pain that each small area of my body felt. My muscles, ligaments, or soft tissues that were affected relived the accident right down to the muscles tensing up as I hit the mat. Most of the time, my lungs relived the accident, along with me not being able to breathe for a few minutes. It was all involuntary. I had no control of it because my mind was handling it.

It took my body years to completely go through and remove the shock from it. My bones were the last to relive the experience. Jack and I witnessed my bones move back into their correct positions on their own. It usually happened when I wasn't feeling any pain or muscle cramps. It would always surprise me to feel something shift when I went to use my muscles. Until I finally felt relief, I didn't realize how much pain that I constantly felt within me. I learned from this experience that shock does not disappear with time.

There are advantages to my body and mind healing from the shock they suffered. My energy is back and I feel more like a teenager than I did in my teens. My shoulders are level and my spine is now straight. You can see my spine all the way down my back. It was hard, but it has been very rewarding. My vision and hearing has improved, along with my digestive system. We've heard for years that our minds can heal ourselves. I've witnessed it and it's marvelous to watch the mind and body work together.

I'm very grateful for all the shock that I've experienced. Each one taught me so much about how we are put together. With the shock removed, I found love. For the first time, I could experience it from others, besides myself. With the numerous layers of shock removed, I'm experiencing life with passion. It's nice to stop and smell the flowers that are along my pathway of life.

Today, I'm healthy physically, emotionally, spiritually, and mentally. If I find myself in a new situation, I have peace to know that I can work myself out with ease. I know how to stop the shock from affecting my life. For the first time, I have total freedom.

In the next chapter, I want to talk about unpeeling the layers of scars that might affect you, so you can have peace with your past and understand how humans function. Maybe, it isn't necessary to get upset with those who have been cruel. We all hurt more than what we are dumping on others.

Hopefully, you will have more patience with others. We all have needs. It's wonderful to be able to give them to yourself and you don't have to wait for someone else to give it to you. My hope is that you can finish this book and learn how to love yourself. Remember, you can only feel love, according to what you can feel yourself.

Chapter 11

Unpeeling the Layers

I giggled in the movie *Shrek* when I heard the title character compare himself to an onion. We all have layers that we've built our lives upon. I've devoted a chapter on this subject because sometimes the layers of our lives aren't what we want. Like an onion, some of the layers might not smell the best and we need to peel them off.

Some of the different layers could be frozen moments of shock, while other layers might be mistakes we made, fears, addictions, or negative decisions. Causing our lives to be governed by these layers can override a new decision that we make today. I'm going to talk about these layers. In another chapter, I'll show you how to remove the negative decisions and replace them with positive, alternative choices.

One thing that can cause layers within us is addiction. There are numerous ways to become addicted. In my life's story, I mentioned my father being addicted to the emotion of sympathy. Jen and Aunt Janice were addicted to praise. My grandmother was addicted to anger and hate in her life. There are numerous emotions that you can become addicted to.

You can become addicted to any emotion you want. For an example, some people choose to become addicted to the gratification of power. When they do, they become addicted to manipulating others and also become controlling without little thought. They will try to use their power to manipulate any situation. It becomes a game for them that they dearly love. Usually, we aren't aware of being controlling and in the process we can hurt others deeply. Not realizing it, we mostly hurt ourselves.

This is how we can become addicted to our own emotions. Every time we have a thought, our emotions translate the thought into a feeling. It means our emotions have changed the thought into a chemical so the body can feel it. During the moment of feeling that emotion, you can believe that you either really like this feeling or hate it. Either way, the mind reads hate or love as the same. It thinks you want this emotion in your life and the mind likes to please you. The downside is the mind doesn't understand consequences.

If your mind believes that you love the emotion, then it will cause you to be addicted to the chemical the emotion has created. Now, your mind will repeat the emotion often for you. If you really hated it, you now have a problem.

Here are some of the different emotions you can become addicted to:

- Love or Hate
- Fear and Worry
- Jealousy
- Lust

There are more. I picked a few just to give you an idea of how it happens. When your mind chooses to make you addicted, it can affect you greatly. Some people will allow addictions to control their lives. I want to talk about how each one of the above emotions can affect your behavior and decisions.

Love or Hate

I've already explained that the two emotions are the same as far as the mind is concerned. They just happen to be at opposite ends of the spectrum. Love or hate is attached to everything we do and say. It's the constant basis of every thought. The emotion dictates our perception of a given situation. First off, let's talk about love.

There are people so addicted to love that they instantly become attention-seekers, wanting to find love from others. We've all seen the criminal who wants their picture on the news to the point that they even lie about doing a crime just to get the attention. What we don't realize is this kind of attention is very fleeting.

Attention is a basic need that all of us have. We'll run around throughout life, wanting people to give it to us. What we don't realize is the kind of attention we hunger for needs to come from within. We need to put our arms around ourselves and say, "I love you. You're going to be okay. We're going to get through this together."

Therefore, you need to love yourself first before you can truly love and feel loved from someone else.

The emotion of hate also brings forth many consequences.

Hate can lead to anger and resentment. It's resentment that really damages our immune system. When we are full of resentment, we aren't aware of the flowers that are along the path of life and, as a result, our perception of life is warped.

We've all heard the saying, "Love is blind." Hate being the same emotion is very blind. With hate, we see what we only want to see and become blind to new ways of thinking, even if they are right. Therefore, negative emotions stop us from seeing the truth in all things. When we choose negative emotions, we bring towards us people who are angry and resentful. If you find this happening in your life, and you want them to stop coming into your life, you can stop them by changing your thoughts from negative to positive.

Fear and Worry

All of us have fear within us to one degree or another. Fear is usually trapped in your moments of shock. When we experience fear, we promise to never allow it to happen again. This is why we worry. It's the fear we have associated to a moment and our minds are trying to protect us. What our minds don't understand is in the process of protecting us, they're bringing us exactly what we do not want.

We already know what fear can do to us. It stops us from enjoying life and it can cause diseases. Fear deteriorates our immune system.

Robert told us that fear can cause some types of flu. Not sure about this, I pondered on my past. I would get the flu four to six times a year. I could see it definitely happened during an event that added to my fears frozen in time.

In high school, I was afraid to speak in front of people for many reasons. If I had to do something where I would be judged, I would lose my voice every time. We all know why I had the fear of being judged for communicating. It didn't ever stop me from giving my speech. Losing my voice gave me a good excuse for doing a poor job.

Remember, worry is our mind trying to protect us from having another bad experience. However, it only brings you what you don't want. In the end, fear and worry make us believe we can't do something when, in fact, we can.

Jealousy

This is a dangerous emotion and I would make it a rule to never allow yourself to have it. When we feel jealousy, we have the thought that we can't do or have something that someone else has or can do. People can actually become addicted to this emotion. They often blame or ridicule others out of jealousy. When we blame others for our lot in life, it means we are terrified to look at ourselves. It means we do not love ourselves.

In some ways, jealousy is a form of hate. There are people who steal from others simply because they hate that they have something they do not. Stealing takes away from your self-love and self-worth. Nothing will destroy this other than stealing, lying, or cheating. And, in this way, jealousy can affect our moral judgment.

In Chapter Fifteen, you'll learn how this emotion stops us from having what we want.

Lust

Lust is an easy emotion to become addicted to. It's the first emotion that we feel when we see nudity. Today, we see nudity everywhere and even as a child we'll feel a certain level of lust. The addiction to this emotion usually comes from pornography, revealing dress in public, and in entertainment. When our minds hear us say we like the feeling of lust, the mind will create a desire within us to want more.

To add to the problem, nudity causes shock within our minds. It's the same shock you felt with the nine-eleven attacks or when President Kennedy was killed. The moment is frozen in our minds. When we repetitiously see nudity, we are reinforcing the addiction to lust.

This addiction can fit into committing adultery. We can become addicted to the thrill of getting away with something or doing something forbidden. To feed that addiction, there are men and women who cheat on their spouses.

Now, you understand why this addiction causes good people to do bad things. They are ashamed of it later. We've all seen how it destroys people's lives and their families.

How do you change the addictions?

I found several ways of doing it. The best way is to ask your mind to go to the origin of when you first had the thought that you want to change. Once you are there, ask your mind to go back five minutes before. The feeling from the thought should feel differently.

Now this is your time to change how you feel about the thought. I would tell your mind that you do not want to become addicted to the emotion that thought creates. When you feel peacefulness, then focus on associating this feeling to the thought every time you have the thought in the future. Remember, you have to think first about everything that has happened or come into your life.

In the next chapter, I'm going to talk about all the different ways of changing your habits. Maybe, you'll find one that will help you.

Chapter 12

This Is What I Learned

It's a thrilling day when I learn something new. I feel successful. In life, we all need to decide what success means to us. Some people will set their success on how much money they can make. In my life, I set a goal to learn something new each day. This is my definition of a successful day. Every day, I can feel successful. When you feel successful, you appreciate your life and have fun.

If you don't make a conscious choice, your mind will make one for you by listening to your words. Sometimes, the decision is so lofty you seldom feel successful.

Success is a habit that you need to feel each day. It was like me learning to speak at the age of eighteen months. We all needed to feel successful. Just once, if someone made me feel successful when my father was telling me I couldn't communicate properly, it could've overridden what he did to me.

You need to feel successful every day. I've heard some people express that they are successful just by being above the ground. For me, I needed something else. In my heart, I would rather be with my mother, so I had to find something else that would be meaningful to me.

Why is it so important to feel success?
When you feel success, you build confidence and this is important. It's a positive thought. When the thought changes into a feeling, then you'll bring success towards you. This is what we all want, so be smart and

do not make success hard for you to find. Always remember, you need to be patient.

We want to have positive thoughts with us at all times.

Our attitudes are everything in our lives. Attitudes are feelings we have towards everything in our lives. We attract other people, events, and things that we focus on. If you want to know what you are thinking, you need to look at your attitude.

For example, some people dislike exercising. Somewhere, they've programmed their minds that it's unpleasant. In doing so, they never get the benefits out of exercising. It produces endorphins within the body that makes you feel good. It relieves stress. If someone's attitude is negative, can they exercise and enjoy it? No.

I want to talk about how a thought translates into a feeling. Let's say, one day you decided as a kid that you don't like to swim. Someone had pushed you into the water when you weren't ready and it frightened you. In anger, you tell yourself that you do not like to swim. Your emotions take the thought and change it into a chemical so your body can feel it. If you allow the anger to stay, you will have a hard time ever enjoying swimming. You might have set yourself up to miss a wonderful experience. You can even become afraid of the water. Yet, you have nothing strong to base your fear upon.

Is the water really going to hurt you? Does the water hurt your skin when you touch it? It's the negative possibilities that you have anchored to swimming. Maybe, you would enjoy snorkeling in the Caribbean, but the fear of water stops you from really enjoying a new world and having wonderful memories. What have you stopped yourself from really enjoying in life because of an innocent decision that your mind held you to?

Can you reverse these decisions?

Yes, you can. I've learned you can tell your mind to go to the origin of the decision and reverse it so you can enjoy swimming in water.

You can tell your mind to replace the decision with the enjoyment of swimming. Then tell yourself that you always want to feel this way in the present and future.

If you did it right, you should feel good about swimming. If you don't, then it means that you have shock attached to swimming. So you'll need to go back and put your arms around yourself and say that you're okay. Just hold yourself mentally, until you feel the fear and shock melt away. When you feel fear from your past, it's usually associated to shock.

I learned the mind stores our decisions and memories in different areas of our bodies. If they are negative, our decisions can cause diseases or problems within our bodies. Let me give you an example. I made a decision that I didn't want to see my future. I felt there was nothing to look forward to. My mind took the decision, changed it into a chemical, and stored it in my eyes.

Now, I can't see in the distance without using glasses. I made my decision to stop hoping for the future. It happened when my father forced me to take care of myself in my senior year. Some time after I started my senior year, my eyesight grew weaker. Looking back, my eyes started to mutate themselves to match my decision. My eyes became blurry and I couldn't see the blackboard. With my income, I couldn't afford glasses. So I compensated by asking the person next to me to tell me what was on the board.

Like most women, my eyes became worse with each child. By the time I had my third child, the eye doctor told me my new prescription was considered for the legally blind. When I picked up my new pair, I was frustrated to see my lenses resembled the thickness of a soda bottle bottom. They hurt the bridge of my nose with their weight.

Two months later, they came out with plastic lenses. Quickly, I changed my glasses. The bridge of my nose was very happy to have plastic lenses. Today, my eyes are reversing themselves. They have improved by seven steps. My glasses are slowly sliding down my nose so I can see my computer better. When they reach the end of my nose, I know it's time to get a new prescription. My eyes are getting better as I heal from my past and change my thoughts.

This is what happened to me. In a book, I found this:

Stigmatism

We made the decision to be afraid of seeing ourselves.

Cataracts

We expressed an inability to see ahead with joy. Dark future.

Farsighted

Fear of the present.

Nearsighted

Fear of the future.

When I read this, I had stigmatism and was nearsighted. I felt the same way the examples expressed. You can judge it for yourself. I wouldn't be surprised if my eyes became normal and I could see perfectly without glasses. I need to make sure an improper thought doesn't start to cause problems. It's well worth the effort to go back and clean out the negative thoughts.

Another problem I had was suffering from mild hyperglycemia. I found it to come and go. In a book, it pointed out that hyperglycemia and diabetes could be caused by our thoughts. The thought is stored in the gland that makes our insulin:

Diabetes

Longing for what might have been. A great need to control. Deep sorrow. No sweetness left.

From what I have been told, hyperglycemia is a forerunner for diabetes. On the above statement, I felt **no sweetness left in life**. The other statements meant nothing to me. I noticed I had problems with hyperglycemia when I was feeling **no sweetness left in life**. If I was feeling it, then it means I thought it. My body manifested it by causing me to be hyperglycemic.

We have spent time talking about the mind, body, and emotions, but very little about the spirit. **The spirit is a fascinating part of the equation and the most misunderstood part of us.** It means a lot to me to be talking about the spirit. I never would've understood the spirit if I hadn't seen for myself how damaged mine was.

When Jack made me stand in front of the mirror, and the invisible arms joined him, I saw how thick the layers of shock were within my spirit. Like a laser, I felt Him cut through the scars so I could feel His love for the first time since my mother died. It stung for a moment and then His love felt very soothing. I was stunned to understand how hard it was for me to feel His love. For the first time, I really felt Jack's love, along with His.

I want to talk in depth about our spirits. First, we all know our bodies would dry up and turn to dust without our spirits. Just like our bodies, our spirits can shrivel up if they aren't nourished properly. It's a common problem to **not** take care of our spirits. You want your spirit strong.

Why is it important to have our spirits strong?

Out of the four areas of the mind, body, spirit, and emotions, one needs to be the boss. When the spirit is weak, our bodies, minds, or emotions will take over as the leader. The strongest one will take over and it's usually the body. The mind, emotions, and body have no clue about the consequences of your actions.

The mind only sees one-dimensionally. It doesn't see around the corner, nor does it understand consequences. Emotions are the same way. The mind, emotions, and body react while the spirit is proactive. The three also gravitate to the negative. The spirit is the only part that aches for positive thoughts and feelings.

Nourishment for the spirit is love. In my case, I couldn't feel it from all of the shocked moments of being abused. You also need to understand how to give yourself love. As you can see, it's so easy to have self-love taken away. It's hard to love yourself, unless you learn how. We are taught from birth to love ourselves. This is why I've dedicated a whole chapter to it.

How do we feed the spirit to keep it in charge?

Your spirit thrives on a very special love. It only comes from one place: You! We need to learn to give ourselves unconditional love. This is the most powerful love in the universe. It's a taught love and when you master unconditional love, life is wonderful and your spirit thrives on it. No one can give it to you, but yourself.

When you were born, you loved yourself. However, in this life, we are taught to not love ourselves. The first time we are criticized, humiliated, or we make a mistake, we stop loving ourselves and the problems begin. With self-love stopped from coming to our spirits, they start to become weak.

With self-love gone, your spirit weakens, allowing one of the other areas to take over. When they take over, you have chaos. They are always reacting to every negative thought around you. Then you attract negative people, events, and things into your life that aren't pleasant. You've probably heard of the cliché, "birds of a feather flock together." This is a true statement.

Positive and negative people flock together. For some reason, a negative person can clear out a room of positive people. It works that same way. If you find yourself surrounded with negative people, and you want out, then change your thoughts. They'll leave and people with your positive thoughts will come towards you. It's your spirit that gives you the strength to change and learn your way out of a situation. If it's weak, then you'll take a very painful easy way out.

The spirit is the only aspect of you that can guide and heal you through life. We all have problems and we all want to find peace. Remember, everything needs to be created spiritually before it can be manifested. When you were learning to walk, you had to think it out in your mind first. You had to see yourself walking before you could do it.

The spirit is what made it possible.

How do you know if your spirit is in charge?

If you have mastered self-discipline, you know that your spirit is in charge. Self-discipline is a choice and you need to practice it on a constant basis to be good at it. If self-discipline is a new concept, you might want to start with what I did.

Jack and I picked a day once a month to fast for at least twenty-four hours. Sometimes, we don't make it because of our schedules. Most of the time, we do it. I mention our schedules because we try to do as little physical activity as possible during the twenty-four hour period. Instead, we like to read, meditate, or take the time to pay attention to our thoughts. Most of the time, we give so much to other people that we need time to fill our cups.

It's a time to evaluate my life, personal needs, goals, reading material, or thoughts about what I'm grateful for. I like to think about what I'm grateful for or take the time to heal something. This is a time I like to look at my goals and see where I am and how I need to spend my time.

The fasting is a way to take a break from stress. We all live with a certain amount of stress constantly. I think of fasting as taking a vacation and rejuvenating myself. Today, Jack and I still fast once a month. We appreciate this down time.

Speaking of stress, I want to give you another idea on controlling it. **The best way to deal with the stress of life is to have an attitude of gratitude.** It seems strange that an attitude of gratitude will relieve stress, but it does. You've probably heard that exercising relieves stress. This is right. It's the deep breathing that relieves it. So if you aren't into exercising, you might want to breathe deeply at least four times a day. It's very healthy and you have stress under control.

Be appreciative of those who have trespassed against you.

This is another tidbit that I learned that was valuable. It keeps the negative emotions from messing up your life. Being appreciative of your enemies is the most liberating experience you'll ever have. The rewards are worth every moment.

It goes along with loving your trials. I've mentioned this in other chapters. Whatever happens in your life becomes a part of you.

I love history and one of my heroes happened to be Gandhi. He's a good example of someone who knew how to love his enemies and his spirit was in control because of that. He made this choice all along the way. Notice the powerful effect he had on the world.

There's another area I want to take a moment and talk about. How do you feel about your family? Do you have a hard time being around your siblings? If you do, you might want some advice on what could be causing your negative experiences.

First, you are thinking negatively about it. You know for sure they are going to repeat something that offends you. So you join the family function, daring them to repeat what offends you. They probably will do it. It's your fault most of the time. When we picture in our minds how someone is supposed to act, we will be disappointed if a family member doesn't hold up to this image.

Sometimes, we're upset with someone and it's completely based on fantasy and not fact. We can't see into someone's heart or know his or her thoughts. If we love ourselves, it's very easy to accept them. When you accept them, you can talk with them and stand in their shoes. Most of the time, we are frozen in a thought regarding them. Sometimes, they have changed or moved on. If they haven't, your loving them protects you from harboring negative thoughts. A negative thought is lethal to us.

If you truly step back and appreciate your family, you'll learn a lot about yourself. In another chapter, I will explain why in detail. They are a part of you and in loving them, you're giving back to yourself. If I can love my family after what they did, you can.

In my next chapter, I'm going to talk about depression. I gave it a whole chapter because I lived with it for so long and so many suffer from it. There are two thoughts that trigger it and I want to teach you about them.

Chapter 13

Depression

Do you like being depressed? I didn't. It changes the whole perspective of your life. You probably already know about it. I bet everyone has experienced it to one degree or another. We all know how painful depression can feel as it zaps all joy of life from us like a fire will suck out the oxygen that's in a room.

What is depression?

Depression is a byproduct of very negative emotions that have been preceded by thoughts. If the negative thoughts are frozen in a moment of shock, then you can have a serious problem. We've all seen how it can destroy lives if it's left unchecked. This is one reason it's important for you to go back and melt all the moments of shock in your life. Usually, negative thoughts accompany shock and you can see how dangerous it can be.

For me, I found depression very painful and this was due to my childhood. It causes us to become blind to the beauty of the world that's around us. We aren't capable to see life in its true form. Our minds twist our perceptions to fit the frozen feeling of depression.

The emotions that caused my depression were deeply engrained inside of me. When I was an adult, people would talk about depression and I would tell them that I had never felt it. I wasn't lying. To me, I didn't know anything different. It wasn't until I started to melt the shock inside me that I finally had something to compare my life against. Then I realized my spirit was in deep depression.

Like shock, depression doesn't melt away with time. You have to do something. After I left my family's influences, I still suffered. My frozen moments of shock made it impossible to change, until I finally learned how to melt them years later.

If I could do my life all over again, I would've found Robert sooner to melt all of my icebergs at a younger age. Then I could've become my true self and enjoy living for the first time.

What are the emotions that are linked to depression?

Like I've stated before, our emotions get started with a thought. The emotion changes the thought into a chemical so we can feel the emotion. Anytime you accept the thought as being real, you find yourself trapped in an unwanted situation. Depression will consume you, if you repeat certain thoughts numerous times.

Psychiatrist and author Viktor Frankl found this secret. When living in a concentration camp, Frankl let go of his hopelessness and lived, while everyone around him was dying from a broken heart. Their dreams were shattered and they felt betrayed by their country. He refused to feel trapped. You make the choice to not be trapped. When you accept the thought of being trapped, you are quitting. Depression is a byproduct of the emotion and decision to quit. We can do this on a subconscious level.

When you embrace hopelessness, you have given up on your possibilities. If I could go back and do it all over again with what I know today, I would've not quit on hope.

I made the choice to have hope years before I learned how to heal. My deep spiritual depression did not leave me, just because I decided to have hope. When I revisited my memories, I saw that I made my decision to feel trapped based upon shock. It shocked me that my father wouldn't acknowledge my pain.

My perception was he didn't care about me. Jen was just like him. She didn't care, because she had nothing to give with Don verbally abusing her. With Jen not showing any concern for my pain, she helped him cement the abuse inside of me. She became a part of the problem. If she had been truthful with me, she would've helped me.

The advantage of my experience with them was when I removed the scars, the joy of having the pain gone was almost overwhelming. I doubt that I would've appreciated what I learned from Robert without the contrast of the two. It is a powerful lesson that I learned.

What is one thought again that causes depression?

Hopelessness! We are trapped with no choices in an unwanted situation.

Can we change depression just by changing our thoughts?

Yes. It can also have some attachments like shock that can make it hard to just change your thoughts. Some people find depression a problem that plagues them because it runs in their family. It's very possible to pass on the tendency of depression to your progeny.

How can depression be passed down from one generation to another?

There are two ways depression can be passed on to the next generation. One is depression is a taught behavior. Think about it. When you are unsure about how to handle a situation, what do you do? You look to see what other people are doing. If you find yourself in an unsure situation and no one is around, you think back to how you saw someone else handle the same situation.

Let me give you another way we teach our children our fears and unwise choices. Until I learned how to alter my thoughts, I was afraid of heights. Jack was the opposite. Before we had children, he crawled over a guardrail at the Grand Canyon and stood on the very edge so he could look down the deep canyon. If the small rock he stood on couldn't handle his weight, he would've plunged a mile to his death, if he didn't hit more rocks sticking out of the canyon's wall first. Stupid, oh yes. You notice I said he did it before we had any children.

For me, I stand on a kitchen chair and I'll stop breathing and get lightheaded. So when we built our first home, Jack decided to put artificial stones on the outside of our house. To reach everyplace, Jack used two-story scaffolding.

Malcolm and Josh wanted to follow their father up the scaffolding. He said yes and I said no. I said, "Jack, I don't want them to fall and . . ."

He stopped me and responded, "You're not going to teach our boys to be afraid of heights like you."

In my heart, I knew Jack was right. I was taught to be afraid of heights to the point where I could've passed out in seconds by standing on a chair. I would stop breathing from fear, reliving my brother tossing me up in the air. He would tease me that I was going to hit the high ceiling of the house.

So I chose to say nothing, watching my two boys follow their father like little puppies. They never fell. More important, Josh and Malcolm aren't afraid of heights. None of my children are afraid of heights because I didn't tell them about all the negative things that could happen. I did teach them some other dumb things that they will need to change.

We can be taught by others around us to quit and give up. It's easy to pass it on by our example. We teach more by our example than we do by our words. I didn't want my children to just accept things as status quo. It's important we teach our children to think their way out of a situation.

I punished my children by sending them to their room. They could come out immediately, but they had to tell what they did to contribute to the problem. They needed to explain how they were going to change their actions in the future, so they wouldn't keep the problem coming into their lives.

With them now being adults, I watch them work through their problems a lot faster than I did. Sometimes they amaze me. We do teach our children our thought patterns of negative or positive. It's interesting to watch families. I'll see some families where all of the children make a decision based upon fears. It's interesting to watch them. They make the simplest decision by placing fear in the equation to justify making the decision.

What should you do if you're not happy with the behavior you picked to copy?

Ask your mind to go back to the origin of when you made a decision to copy that person. When you see it in your mind, you need to mentally put your arms around yourself and say, "I'm from the future and it was a mistake to copy that person's behavior. It's okay you made a mistake. I love and forgive you. What I need is for you to make this choice. Will you do it?"

You should feel a yes or no from yourself. When you feel the yes, you say, "Are you willing to replace it?" You should feel a yes. Then you ask to replace that behavior with a positive one and send it into the future. You'll feel the change and when you do, thank your younger self and leave.

There is another way depression can be passed on to our progeny. In some families, they will find a tendency to feel depressed, suffer from diseases, or even become an alcoholic. Everything can't be a taught behavior. So what happens? I told you about the body storing our decisions. Sometimes, our chemical decisions get attached to our DNA and we pass it on to our progeny. This is why you can watch siblings put butter on their slices of toast exactly the same way. In my case, my sister Mary and I didn't like to eat ice cream. How did this happen? We didn't live with each other. Somewhere, our ancestors made a decision to not like ice cream and for some reason it became dominant with Mary and me. Jen loves it.

Can you change an ancestor's decision from affecting you?
How do you know it's an ancestor's decision?

Yes, you can change your ancestor's decision from affecting you. Let's talk about how to know if it's an ancestor's decision first. Ask your mind to go to the origin of a decision. If you can't see it in your mind, then it means you are experiencing someone else's decision.

You need to tell your mind to go back to the first time you ever liked or disliked something. Ask your mind to sever the feeling so you aren't feeling it anymore. The mind will do what you ask.

Let me give you an example. Somewhere in my family, a person made a decision to crave sugary foods. I couldn't find a place where I made that decision. So I asked my mind to sever the craving. My mind did it and the craving went away.

Can this technique work for being addicted to drugs, smoking, or alcohol?

I have never had the problem with alcohol, drugs, or smoking. So I cannot tell you if it would work. It would be interesting to see if it would work. If I were someone who had a problem, I would try it. What do you have to lose? I would also like to know if it worked.

If you are thinking about doing it, let me give you a little more information. Sometimes, we link other reasons for having problems. For an example, we might be overweight for emotional reasons and not necessarily crave food. Or you could have both problems.

You can possibly change it with this technique. Just realize that there might be ten other reasons coming together to create your problem. It will take you going through all ten reasons to change it. For me to change what my father did so I could communicate clearly, I had to fix between ten to fifteen areas. My mind had linked the experience to other issues.

For an example, I linked fear that everyone would do what my father did to me. So performing in front of people terrified me. When I tried to write, I had to remove all of the imaginary areas that I thought might hurt me in the future. My mind was trying to protect me by attaching my fears to other situations. We are complex. Be patient and keep turning over stones until you get the results you want. There is never one magic bullet.

Have you heard the cliché "We need to realize that we become like the people we associate with"? I bring this up because I hope you can see that you need to be careful whom you choose to be your close friends. You become like them if you're not consciously telling yourself what you see with them is acceptable or unacceptable behavior. This is important. I've mentioned that my siblings became like those they lived with.

You also need to be careful about what kind of information you put into your mind. **How do I keep my thoughts in control or checked?** This is the place and time for **affirmations**. It helps to say, "I'm grateful that I can always make a positive choice in any situation. I'm grateful to have such an abundant future and I'm wise with my money." You can go on with what you want to have yourself feel and believe. It's important to tell yourself to find the positive side of every situation. Why? You give yourself hope and eliminate the trapped feeling from your life.

Negative thoughts pull you into feeling trapped and hopeless. Keep positive words in front of you. **There is always a way out of every situation. You always have a choice.** Even with my grandmother and the others in my family, I always had a choice to how I felt about my situation. One thing I did that saved me from behaving like them was I made a decision to view the negative behavior as being unacceptable. I didn't choose to hate because I knew that I would lose the invisible arms around me. I needed Him desperately. Being free of hate, I wasn't blinded, but instead I had knowledge of what was going on around me. It didn't keep me from being angry. I had a lot of anger pent up inside of me.

I wished I understood years earlier how powerful being grateful could be in your life. Be grateful for your joys, trials, and sorrows and they will all come and go throughout your life. They have value when you learn to love them all. The bad times teach you how wonderful the good times can be for you. By loving your trials, it will soften the pain.

Your thoughts are everything, as you can see. Is it a surprise? It was to me to see how powerful our minds and words are to us. This is why our words can inflict severe pain to others and us. If you find yourself inflicting pain on others, stop it now and you might want to find out what's behind your abuse.

Remember, you're only doing it because you do not love yourself. We are showing to the world how we feel about ourselves. Some people think they can bluff their way through life. People can see who you really are if they want to. By loving yourself, you will be able to give love to others. You can have a powerful impact on others just with a genuine smile.

We can't give what we don't have. So fill your cup and it will make your life wonderful. In the next chapter, I'm going to talk about self-love and self-worth. We might be repeating some ideas, but it is okay. Self-love and self-worth are the cornerstones of your life.

Chapter 14

Self-Worth and Love

Self-worth is something that most of us cry out for when we aren't feeling it. We keep looking at everyone to validate us. Yet, what we don't understand is people can't give validation to us when we need it. Sometimes, they can't because they don't feel it themselves. You can't give something that you don't have.

Another reason is that sometimes they are too caught up in their own lives to give it. Some people will give it to you, but you might struggle to feel it when they do. Why? You have to give it to yourself to feel it from others. No matter how you look at it, you must accept yourself first.

Self-worth is a byproduct of self-love. We need to have self-love in place first to feel self-worth. This is why I put them together. They go hand in hand. Since I mentioned you had to feel self-love first, let's talk about it.

What is self-love?

It's how we feel about ourselves. It doesn't mean we are consumed with just our wants and needs. Self-love is purely unconditional love for ourselves. Do you love yourself? Are you pleased with yourself? Or are there things that you wish would melt away?

These feelings never go away and we usually blame others because we are afraid to look at ourselves. It's a wonderful experience to mentally put your arms around yourself and say, "I accept you and everything you have brought into my life."

If you do it from the heart, you should feel a wave of love for yourself and it should bring you to tears. Most of us like to blame others for our problems. When we do this, we are telling the world that we're afraid to look at and accept ourselves.

So we'll belittle someone else. A bully is a person who screams lack of self-love. Belittling someone is a hideous crime. When you see someone do it, then you need to know that they are treating themselves just as badly. We treat people the same way we deal with ourselves.

So if we are lying to ourselves, we will lie to others. Anything negative drains self-love. This is why it hurts in the inside when you first lie. If you keep it up, you'll become numb. There are other behaviors that deplete our self-love. I want to talk about them first. If you aren't aware of what removes self-love, then it will be like a sieve. The love is running out the bottom as fast as you're putting it in.

Taking advantage of someone because they are vulnerable or doing it because you can and the authorities will not penalize you.

Some people will take advantage of anyone, no matter who it is. With a company policy, some people think it's their right to find a way to cheat others. Employees who steal from their companies only end up losing in the end. We've also seen it the other way around when a company lies about their profits and then goes under. Some people think it's a right to take advantage of vulnerable people or their own families.

It's an easy trap to fall into because we aren't taking the time to stand in someone else's shoes. Jack and I set up a strong rule that governs how we do business. We will not complete any kind of business transaction unless it is a win-win situation. This includes going to a grocery store. When you do something dishonest, like keeping the wrong amount of change, you are cheating yourself. I almost want it to happen so I can give it back. It feels so wonderful that I can literally feel love consuming my spirit.

Another action we can do to deplete our self-love, and not realize it, is through **fornication** and **adultery**. You probably will agree that adultery can deplete our self-love because it is cheating on a promise you made to someone else. I bet you're wondering why fornication depletes your self-love. This is the one that I want to talk about.

Today, our society accepts fornication as a right to everyone. Some people take it to the point that they should get it anyway they can. It's talked about in movies and on TV that someone should have it when they want it. Wrong? This is so selfish. It's all about **them**. But some people will say both partners get something out of it. So what's wrong with it?

Fornication affects you the same way adultery does. You're probably wondering where the promise was made to someone else. Before I answer that question, I need to explain how a sexual act affects your mind, body, emotions, and most of all your spirit.

To begin with, let's tear fornication apart. What is the act based upon? Is it based on love or hate? Some people would say love. Let's go deeper. What is the underlying emotion that is present during fornication? **It is pure selfishness**. Each person is looking out for just themselves and what they are going to get out of the two coming together. So the relationship is based on a lie. There is no promise to be loyal to each other.

Some people will argue that their act of fornication is based on love. If you are feeling that way, then you might be lying to yourself. There is a difference between lust and love. It takes time to develop love where lust is fleeting. Most men focus on lust and then reach the stage of love.

How does fornication affect your self-love?

The mind and spirit know this act is meant to bind the two people together for a long time. When the commitment isn't there, the mind and spirit deem it as a lie. With a lie, you lose more of your self-love and you can feel empty soon afterwards. If you keep it up, you can find yourself becoming very numb. It is possible to become addicted to the emotion of lust.

When this happens, you want to feel satisfaction, but you aren't getting it because you're going against what intercourse was meant to be.

So why should you care?

The sexual act is meant to be a **spiritual experience**. When you choose to have fornication, your spirit moves back and if lust is involved, the emotions join the spirit. To have a spiritual experience, you need all four areas participating. You miss the complete bonding experience.

To have a spiritual experience, both partners need to have their minds, bodies, spirits, and emotions come together as one. If one partner is committed and the other isn't, the committed partner can become deeply hurt.

Let me describe what happens during a complete spiritual experience for two people. Your goal is to have both people be completely unselfish and in love with the other person. Fornication is based on selfishness. It's a negative emotion. Let me draw it out for you.

In your mind, I want you to picture a pyramid with three levels. We will call the bottom level physical. The second level, we will call emotional, and the top level is called spiritual. Men function and respond without thought on the physical level. They can go to the next level, but they have to choose to do it. Once men are on the emotional level, then they need to go up to the spiritual level. You are at the top of the pyramid.

Women function automatically on the second level. They have a choice to go down to the bottom or up to the top. I roll my eyes at the way society is teaching women to go down and not up. If you stay on the physical level, the act becomes very mechanical and empty. Even if you are married, you will find it mechanical and empty. You need to come together with the right thoughts and emotions to have a spiritual experience and put passion back into your life.

What is a spiritual experience like?

When a couple reaches a spiritual experience, the moment binds them together. It cements their relationship in every way. The couple has no desire for anyone else. If you separated this couple, and the only way they could reach each other was over a hot desert, then they would crawl on their hands and knees to get to each other. For some reason, they were bound together and a spiritual experience is that powerful.

With this kind of commitment, parents become a strong core of family security. Without parents having regular spiritual experiences, families have built their houses out of sand. The first strong wave and the family is pulled apart. Spiritual experiences preserve each other's self-love and protect them through the storms of life.

Hopefully, you can see that families are being torn apart by fornication or adultery. They both deplete our self-love and worth and make us weak going into a marriage. Some people move on to a new partner, searching for the answers to only find they have compounded. They are looking for someone to give them the spiritual experience, when it's them who need to change so they can have one.

How do you know if you've experienced a spiritual experience with your spouse?

If you're aware of spiritual experiences, you're offended to watch someone else in the act of bonding together. To you, intercourse is sacred because it's a spiritual relationship. It isn't even appreciated when a program or movie talks about fornication as a causal, everyday happening. When it's spiritual, it's sacred.

Another area where you can stop having self-love and self-worth is not forgiving others or yourself. This one can stop you cold in your tracks of being able to feel self-love. If you aren't forgiving, then it means you're holding resentment, anger, or ill feelings. You have moved to the negative end of love. Hate is involved with all negative emotions. So hate depletes your love.

Since I lived with negative thoughts for so long in my early age, it's easy for me to slip into the destructive pattern. So I chose to forgive instantly. If a car cuts in front of me, I forgive on the spot and it doesn't ruin my day. Years ago, it happened with Jack when he would come home frustrated because of the traffic.

I suggested that he should forgive them on the spot. He thought it was dumb, especially when I told him that people would stop cutting him off. Determined to prove me wrong, he took me up and started to forgive people on the spot. He was taken back on how it really minimized others from cutting him off. He came home in a lot happier mood.

Not dressing modestly.

You're probably wondering why this would stop you from giving yourself self-love. It's because of how the mind interprets immodesty or nudity. The mind and spirit interpret nudity with shock. If we happen to have lust in our minds, our emotions anchor the feeling of lust to the shock. As a result, we become consumed with the emotion and desire. This is one way of becoming addicted to lust.

In the process, your mind and spirit don't **respect** the person who is causing you to feel shock. Let me give you an example. In your mind, I would like you to picture a man or woman who you felt a lot of respect for in the public life.

The first person I had respect for in public life was Jacqueline Bouvier Kennedy Onassis. Everyone seemed to hang on every word she expressed. She was considered America's royalty and she was a highly respected woman. I always saw her dressed modestly and she registered in my mind as a woman you respected.

Now, when you have the respected person firmly in your mind, I want you to change their clothes into a skimpy outfit. Did you see a change in your perspective of them? Do you still respect them?

When I do it, suddenly, the person becomes an object with no feelings, talents, or abilities. Our minds automatically see the person having no value and they become a thing to use. Immodesty triggers and stimulates the body; it always has the perspective of negativity.

If you really love yourself, wouldn't you want to be respected? Can you respect yourself when you look in the mirror? As young girls, we think we're getting attention. I want to ask this question. Are you getting the attention as a person with value? Or are you a thing to be used and cast aside? It's in your hands. Immodesty does deplete your self-love.

How do you protect and rebuild your self-love?

Stay positive regarding yourself, others, and your life. Be grateful for your trials, life, and who you are. Remember to put your arms around yourself often, telling yourself that you're okay. Everything is going to be fine today. Keep healing, you'll always stumble over something new to fix. Every time you do this, you will feel better about you and your life.

Believe in you. This was hard for me to learn, but it's so important. Keep telling yourself it's okay to make a mistake. Learn from it so you can move on. Forgive others for what you think they did to you. Do it quickly. Let go of your negative thoughts before they become a part of you.

Once self-love becomes a part of your life, you'll see how wonderful it is to love yourself. You will find an inner joy that I can't put into words. I often think about what it would be like if everyone in the world would become engaged in learning how to love themselves and accept their trials.

This world would be a wonderful place to live in with everyone loving and discovering all the special things about themselves. It saddens me to see so much anger and hate within our world. People are lost, wandering through life. They have no purpose or passion. I really do wish for world peace, but it really needs to start with each one of us.

Can I become happier? If I could go back and change the effects of my decisions, what would I change? This is what I'm suggesting in this book. You can change your past, present, and future by loving yourself and living a life following some basic rules.

Most of us have been made to feel guilty if we love ourselves. It was that way when I was growing up. I think it's changed with my grandchildren as they are being taught tolerance of other people's differences. When we are truly tolerant of others, we are full of self-love. This is good.

Giving Service.

When you give service from the heart, you're building self-love in others and yourself. Look for ways to genuinely give to others and do it without people really knowing about it. Being quiet about the service you give helps to give you a richer experience. Love the people you are servicing. You'll enjoy the experience far more than not.

By giving service, you'll minimize any pain that you might be experiencing. It's the best medication for emotional and spiritual pain I've found. I really appreciated giving service when I was a kid. When I needed to do something for our neighbors to ease my pain of loneliness, it was great!

In our next chapter, I want to go into the depths on how the mind works. This should help you to understand more about what you have between your ears. Hopefully, you can start to have it work for you and not against you.

Chapter 15

How the Mind Works

This is a fun chapter. I think by now we'll all agree how powerful and important the mind is to us. Before, I've mentioned how the mind works. Now, I want to go into the rules the mind follows so you can see how you're innocently undermining yourself.

I've mentioned before that our minds do not understand consequences. You will see it more in this chapter and especially when I talk about core beliefs. Your mind very much wants to please you and it will follow your programming to accomplish what it thinks you want.

How do we program our minds?

We do it by the words we speak. So what are you saying? Let me list some common statements that we all express. It might help you see how you have been programming your mind without even realizing it.

- I feel like I need to criticize my family and those around me.
- I've found that if I place guilt trips on others, it helps me get them to do what I want.
- I have this urge to be judgmental.
- At times, I can speak disparagingly about someone else.

Let's talk about these statements. If we break them down, you can see how you might be programming your mind in certain ways. Before

I start, I want to point out that the mind doesn't understand what is real or fantasy. It takes everything literally. This means you can be watching something in the media and the mind will react to it as if you're really experiencing it.

If we accidentally tell our minds that we want to be happy, then we have the thought of being trapped. Have you changed the programming that you want to be happy? Our minds can become easily distracted and confused, not knowing how to please us.

Criticizing is very damaging. There is no such thing as constructive criticism. It's the fastest way to ruin a relationship. There is a reason why. Every basic need of a human is to feel acceptance and acknowledgement of their feelings. When someone criticizes you, they are pulling your self-love away from you. If you don't know how to give it to yourself, this can permanently damage a relationship or it will over time. We push everyone away from us when we criticize them because it's usually delivered with no love.

When we criticize others, our minds will take our words in and take away from our own self-love. If you want to test this principle, I suggest you stop doing it for one month and compare your life. You will see the changes, according to how much you criticized others.

I've found that if I place guilt trips on others, it helps me get them to do what I want.

When you apply guilt, you could be doing some damage to others. I'm talking about purposely applying guilt. For an example, "How dare you do this? Don't you know what it will do to your mother or father?" By purposely using guilt to manipulate others, your mind takes that guilt and applies it onto you.

People might accuse you of applying guilt and you're wondering how they are coming up with that judgment call. It could be you used the word **why**. The mind reads why as applying guilt to a question and this is why people will become touchy when the word is used. It can ruin relationships, if you use it too often.

I have this urge to be judgmental.

Anytime you judge someone, the mind will take that same judgment upon you. It's why the bible will say you become like the ones you judge. You have just programmed the mind to own the judgment you just gave out. So be careful. Do you really want to become like those you judge?

At times, I can speak disparagingly about someone else.

Every time you say something disparaging about someone else, your mind will believe that you like it. Remember, it reads hate and love as the same emotion. So it will take in everything you say and apply it to you. So think twice about talking about anyone in a negative form. I suggest you look at the positive side of others. With our minds taking everything literally, do we really want everything to happen by our words?

So my words really program my mind? This is hard to accept.

Remember, I talked about reversing the effects of my trampoline accident. I asked my mind to focus on my body and reverse the accident. It is happening. Going back to my father, he told me that I was a horrible communicator and it would be impossible for me to get better. I embraced his words by allowing myself to be shocked. If I had blown off my father's words, he would've had no effect on me. At the age I was at, I didn't comprehend that fact. I had no experience to compare it to and I trusted my father.

Have you heard your mind can bring to you what you want?

This is a phrase that a lot of people are talking about from the book, *The Secret*. Some people have told me that they don't think it is true. Let me tell you a story from my life. You can program your mind through your words to bring you what you want. The secret is you don't quit or tell your mind something that will stop it from bringing it to you.

After my mother's death, I became afraid to sleep because of the bad dreams I would have. In the morning, I would wake up shaking because of the dreams. At the time, I felt like my father and grandmother had shoved me out in the middle of winter and dared me to survive with just the clothes on my back. What upset me the most was I believed no one would care if I survived or died. I was fearful for my safety, since it was on my shoulders to protect myself.

At the age of five, I came up with a game, trying to get relaxed enough to fall asleep. Some children would pray for a bike. I prayed for a real horse. While I closed my eyes, I didn't want to think about my fears.

So I would concentrate on what kind of a horse I wanted. Innocently, I pictured an Arabian one. In my picture book, I thought they were beautiful and this was what I wanted. In my mind, I tried to picture my horse right down to the color. I couldn't decide, since there were so many choices. So I decided my horse was going to have tiny dots of brown, white, and black.

Every night, I would picture my horse with the meshed colors of black, brown, and white in my mind until I would fall asleep. My heart would ache for this horse to become real. I do not remember how many years I did this. Eventually I stopped, but never told myself that I would never have it.

Twenty-five years later, Jack and I moved into a house with acreage. My neighbor happened to be selling his two horses. He wanted me to buy the mare. I wanted the stallion. As a little girl, my horse was always a stallion. I learned about my neighbor wanting to sell his horses from his wife. We had become friends.

Since we had just moved into a new house that we had just built, we didn't have any savings to buy the horse. The neighbor agreed to sell the horse on monthly payments. He kept the horse until I had him paid for. Right before I signed the contract, he had him gelded and broken to a saddle.

The horse was a registered Arabian. He was young and black with a little white on his face. Soon after I purchased him, he started to change colors. The black started to fade. His mane, lower legs, and tail stayed black. The rest turned into white, brown, and gray small dots. The tail developed numerous silver streaks in it. They call it a rose color or a gray. I was stunned to see him turn into the very horse I imagined as a frightened five-year-old.

Even his personality was like what I had pictured. He was affectionate to me and communicated to me. I could ask him a question and he would nod his head or shake it, letting me know his answer. When my kids rode him, I would tell him what I wanted him to do and he would do it. He filled everything that I had envisioned as a five-year-old.

At another time in the second grade, I drew a picture in class of a horse. I do remember looking at my finished product and saying that this was what I wanted in a real horse. He was brown with four white socks on his feet.

Mary found my crayon picture of this horse in our father's things. I apparently had left it at our grandparents' home and they saved it. I was pleased my father also saved it. She handed it to me because I had my name on it.

When she handed it to me, Mary said, "This horse looks exactly like your horse, Socks." Studying the picture, I realized that she was right. It was Socks. Today, you can find a crayon picture of a second-grader hanging in my office. It's a reminder to me how important it is to visualize our goals. It's a symbol that your mind does bring to you what you want if you're patient.

This is the job of your mind to bring towards you what you focus on. So it's important that you do not undermine yourself by programming your mind to bring you a horse and then later tell yourself that you can't have one. Your mind will stop bringing what you want towards you. Also, you need to make sure your mind is very clear on what you want.

Since I couldn't make up my mind on the color of my first horse, he became all the colors I thought about. It's important you become very specific with your mind. It has a hard time dealing with generalities.

How do you know if you've programmed your mind to take you in the direction you want?

You will want to pay attention to your feelings. Every time I ever thought about a horse, I received a peaceful feeling. It meant that I hadn't done anything to block it from happening. If I had felt pain, sadness, or indifference, then it would've meant I blocked my horse from coming to me.

Pay attention to how you feel. If you feel depressed, then it means you had thoughts of hopelessness or thoughts of being powerless. Every time, your feelings will let you know where you are at with your thoughts. Your feelings did not just appear out of nowhere. They came from some place and for a reason.

If you find it hard to keep track of your feelings, you might want to keep a journal of them and nothing else. This helped me to understand what I was bringing into my life. You can keep a journal for different issues and I kept one for my feelings, so I could monitor my thoughts. It helped me to step back and look at myself a lot easier.

Did I feel fear, anger, or hopelessness this day? Or did I feel joy or happiness while doing nothing really significant? Either way, I could go back and find out what my thoughts were. Every time, the thoughts preceded my feelings and it became a great learning tool for me. Today, I still write my feelings in a journal. It's a very valuable tool for me and I appreciate doing it.

Patience is a virtue for successful people.

With every shattered dream I had given up on, I accidentally did something right when it came to horses. I learned a lot because of it. Sometimes, it's hard to be patient. This is why I like my crayon picture of Socks years before I bought him. Sometimes, we make a mistake to believe that if something doesn't happen within a certain space of time, it won't ever happen.

The minute we say or think our dreams aren't coming, we've just told our minds to stop bringing it towards us. If we become bitter about it, we blame everyone around us when the real person who stopped it was us all along. Watch your words. You'll probably find it interesting exactly what comes out of your mouth when you start to pay attention to it.

How does our minds develop?

Like a healthy body, our minds are always evolving or developing their ability to understand. With age, we can look back and see the different steps our minds took as our views changed. At different ages, our minds will start to develop an understanding of life that wasn't there before. A healthy mind will shift gears so it can comprehend our lives differently.

Below, I've listed the major times in our lives when a healthy mind shifts into another level of understanding:

- Two years old
- Eight years old
- Sixteen years old
- Thirty years old
- Forty years old
- Sixty years old

Let's discuss the various stages of development in great detail, so you can understand why the different ages are major developments for your mind. This is what I found in my research and there is probably more.

I asked different people all the time if they experienced what I did when I arrived at these different stages in life. So far, everyone I asked agreed with me.

Two years. This is the age we started to compare ourselves with those around us. We look at the adults and decide how we will look and behave when we get older. Many decisions are made at this age that totally control our lives. We will talk about this in depth in the next chapter.

Eight years. For some reason, our minds start to understand the difference between right and wrong at this age. Suddenly, it all becomes very clear and comes into focus. It's fun to watch my grandchildren reach eight. Suddenly, they become the police, informing the younger kids what is wrong or right.

It's very important what you teach your children before the age of eight. Whatever they learned before is how they govern their lives and they'll struggle to change it. If we allow our children to build their foundations for life on the sand, their lives will crumble when the storms of life come in on them. It's important we build them on solid rocks so they can stand firmly when the storms hit them. When the challenges come, your children won't crumble.

One thing we can count on is that we will have storms come into our lives that will rattle every part of us. Are we preparing our children to think their way out and make wise choices? Are your children being presented with wise choices by the media? Your children need to know how you feel about what is going on around them. If you're watching something violent on TV, and keep silent, will they think you agree with what is happening? They can't guess what we are thinking.

Sixteen years old. At this age, your mind starts to understand the consequences of decisions, behaviors, and their choices. Before the age of sixteen, you might think you understand the total ramifications of life, but there is so much you really aren't aware of. Suddenly, we feel smarter. It's a new feeling to us and we think no one has gone through it before. We can look at our parents and other adults and judge them to be naïve.

For some reason, we experience a new feeling for the first time. The feeling could be negative or positive. This is why parents roll their eyes when their kids reach this age.

With a new world of understanding being open to us, we start to see life with new eyes and this is good. We grow so much during this time. This is the time to build confidence in our abilities. We've heard some say that teenage years can be so hard on the parents.

If a teen has been taught well, this stage of life doesn't have to be hard on either the parents or their son or daughter. It should be a time where you start to blossom and discover your abilities. You will discover everything, but you should find enough to work on to develop. If you're a hard worker, there is nothing you can't accomplish in your life.

Thirty years of age. This is an age where you finally understand how the adult world works and you start to relax. In your twenties, you're very critical of everyone that matters to you. It's because you're trying to understand by comparing people's methods of living their lives.

During the age of twenty, you're exposed to numerous methods of doing the same thing. Before, you might have only known about two or three. Now, you see many methods and they seem to work for other people. You can become confused as you try to figure out where you fit into the adult world. Some people adjust faster than others into the world of adults. Some people easily see where they fit into as some really struggle with this age.

The age of **forty** is the one I like so far. By entering this age, your mind suddenly seems to become clear again. Suddenly, I started to experience true wisdom for the first time and I liked it. We have put in our dues enough to understand the lessons from life and how important they truly are. We can feel it and it's wonderful to have it a part of us.

Sixty is the next one. Since I haven't reached it yet, I've interviewed others and I seem to get the same answer from them. I learned they started to appreciate life's lessons at this stage. They can comprehend the value of simple moments and how important relationships truly are. Things usually drift away from being that important. This is why people look forward to traveling. They enjoy watching their grandchildren as they discover their world around them. It reminds you of days that seemed like yesterday.

This could be the age where you start to develop regrets. If you find yourself there, please put your arms around yourself and say, "It's okay. Let's find a way to still accomplish what we want to do." Some people tell me that they start to really cherish the true values in their lives and they start to think about slowing down and how they want to do it.

I noticed them mellowing at this age. What they used to get upset with doesn't matter anymore. Some people, I've noticed, either become happier or bitter about their lives. Whatever they were hiding seems to come out at this age. It makes me wonder, how will I be? Will I be happier or bitter? Time will tell.

There might be other stages of development, like eighty for an example. I stopped asking people after they reached sixty. It would be interesting to find out. It's hard to find enough people to give you the answer. For some reason, I wasn't interested in expanding the research past sixty.

I want to summarize what I've learned about the mind:

- It works like a computer and it's one-dimensional and doesn't understand the long-term consequences of its decisions. Your mind will create events in your life that it perceives you want. For an example, if we are afraid of getting into car accidents, most likely we will have numerous car accidents.

- Our fears hold in our minds what we don't want and our minds believe that we do want it. Whatever you focus on, it will bring it to you. Thus, I would rid myself of the shock first. Usually, we aren't interested in bringing in more of what shocked us. By removing the negative shock, we will eliminate some of our fears. Usually, fear is attached to shock.

- We program our minds with our words. It's important to talk kindly about everyone you meet so your mind doesn't copy the traits of individuals that you don't like. You become like those you criticize, persecute, or judge harshly. This is a trap that I would go to lengths to avoid. It's so easy to be critical with others.

- Remember, your mind changes your decisions into chemicals and stores them around your body. For an example, you'll make the decision, *I'm longing for what might have been and I want to control my life so I can bring it back. In deep sorrow, I tell my mind in words that there is no sweetness left in life.* The mind stores it with the pancreas. Now, your gland doesn't produce enough insulin and you have diabetes or hypoglycemia.

- You can also program your glands to produce too much insulin and store it within your body. Again, it will usually do it within the stomach area. Some people have the problem of their bodies storing it inside the fat around the stomach area. So your body

has to produce the fat to compensate for the extra insulin it is storing.
- **What happens when you or your children witness something that is wrong? Do you stay silent or speak up?** They need to hear you tell them that what they are seeing is unacceptable behavior. Our minds need to hear the same thing. Your children and your mind need to hear what you think is proper behavior, especially when you see it.
- If you don't say anything, your children and your mind might believe the behavior is acceptable. Your children need to hear your opinion and they need to see you back up what you say by not doing it. This is the time for them to decide how they will choose to structure their lives. Hopefully, they will pick wisely.

The mind is a wonderful computer. It needs to be respected. What you put into your mind becomes you, so be careful. Seek positive things, so your mind will focus on them and bring positive moments in your life.

Move away from the negative and know that the mind learns by comparing. Like the octopus that I talked about in the introduction of this book, we learn by watching how others handle a situation and we'll copy them automatically unless we stop ourselves from doing it.

In my next chapter, I'm going to talk about the two-year-old. This is a very important age because it has a powerful impact on our lives.

Chapter 16

How to Change a Core Belief

What is a core belief?

When I first heard the phrase, I wondered what it really meant. Why did it have a separate name? To me, a belief was just a belief and you could change it anytime you wanted to. It wasn't until I took classes on thought patterns when I understood how a core belief worked. Now, the word made sense to me. A core belief has defined powers that aren't easily changed.

The definition of a core belief is **an original belief that governs your life's decisions.**

It's sad but true that our core beliefs control our lives with an iron fist. They are the very first decisions we make regarding how to handle different aspects of our lives. Our minds run everything through them and we can't change that fact. Your core belief or decisions determine how you feel and react to every situation that comes into your life.

We're all born with a clean piece of paper in our heads that has nothing written on it. The paper is there for us to decide how we are going to deal with our lives. We make decisions regarding foods, things we like to play with, and what kind of a person we want to be when we grow up. Our decisions are based on what we see or hear around us.

Not knowing any better, we start to formulate our decisions around the words we hear and the behaviors we see in others. For an example, we made the decision if we're going to be thin or fat when we become adults. Most of our core beliefs are made between the ages of one day to five years of age. The majority is made during the age of eighteen months to three.

As we grow, we decide how we're going to approach our lives. For an example, we choose to like music, dancing, and many more things during this time. At a very young age, you become the architect of your life. We pick by doing the very same thing that the octopuses did on Jay Leno's show. After we make our first decision, then we build from there.

This fragile existence we're born into is totally new and we have such little knowledge regarding it. Yet this is the time we decide how we're going to live our lives. It's amazing how little knowledge we have regarding our existence at this time. Yet, we're making decisions that will govern our complete lives.

How do our core beliefs govern our lives?

If you tell your brain that you don't like peas at a young age, do you find it easy as an adult to like them? Do you have a reason for not liking them? Most of the time, we can't explain why, but we really don't like them. It was a core belief and they don't change. Our minds will go to that decision every time to determine how we should feel about them. Our emotions are a reflection of our thoughts.

Why can't we will a core belief to change?

It's your foundation. Let's look at your beliefs like building a wall out of bricks. If you keep changing the size of the bricks, are you going to have a strong wall? The mind likes consistency and sameness. Remember, it works like a computer and it will always go back to the original decision and hold fast to it.

Right now, I want to show how our core beliefs affect us. Then I will show you how to change a core belief and not have your wall crumble. Just like a computer, you can change it and I'll explain later how to do it. I want to discuss how we make our decisions and how they affect our lives.

To give you one example, I want to go back to the story about my father making fun of my speech. He picked the worst time in my existence to traumatize me. The shock cemented my core decision that I couldn't express my thoughts and feelings. So he buried that inside of me.

Sometimes, we can do the same things to ourselves. I could've told myself that I couldn't speak when I found people not understanding me the first time. At two, we start to understand the meaning of words. We'll create our decisions based on our perceptions of what we think is going on around us. Sometimes, we choose a core belief that isn't the best. If we had more understanding of this world, we probably would've made a different choice. What we choose to be our first decision is how we go through the rest of our lives. With these choices, we learn our way out of a situation.

How do you identify your core belief?

Before my Thought Pattern Management classes, I found it hard and confusing to identify my core beliefs. In my class with Robert, he taught me how to recognize them.

There are different ways of finding your core beliefs. In class, Robert had us write down what we wanted. He gave us a minute and it felt like an hour. I couldn't write a word. Embarrassed, I just put down two words and I can't even tell you what they were. After the minute passed, he asked us to write down what we didn't want. My hand flew.

Most of us know what we don't want, but we seldom know what we want. For me, I found it easy because of all the frozen moments of shock. Our minds know exactly want we don't want. People who do not have a lot of moments of shock understand exactly what they want.

Now, you have this list of things you don't want. You need to pick one and ask your mind to take you back to the origin of that decision. You should be able to see the age and circumstances that you were at when you made the decision. When your mind takes you back to the origin of a decision, it shows you the very first time you decided to make a judgment call regarding this subject.

For an example, I will tell you how I erased my father's ill-effects when trying to get me to speak correctly. In my mind, I would watch the scene play out and I started to put donkey ears on him to make the moment lighter for me. Then I would ask my mind to speed up the scene quickly.

When I felt I was through it, I asked my mind to play it backwards. Usually, it's very funny and that's what you want. Ask your mind to play it forward and backwards until it looks so ridiculous you start to laugh. When you can laugh at the moment, you have erased the shock.

You should also have a good feeling. Now, I asked my mind to go to the beginning of when my father first paid attention to my ability to speak so fast. I said, "I chose to be an excellent speaker. I can communicate with clarity and make it easy for others to understand and follow me."

If your spirit agrees with you, you should expect deep warmth coming from your chest cavity. When you feel it, you need to ask your mind to bring the moment to the present and take it out. Once your mind has done it, you should find yourself letting out a big sigh. You'll want to go back and do it for everything on your list.

I found this to work for the moments where I was traumatized. If you just made a decision that you wish you could go back to, what I just told you about won't work as well. There is nothing to make you laugh. Before I give you a method on how to change those decisions, I want to discuss them first.

What are the different areas in our lives where we all choose to make a core belief?

Am I worthy to be loved?

Every one of us decided if we were going to be worthy to be loved or accepted. We base it on touch or someone doing something for us. We'll base love on people's gifts, words of affirmations, touch, quality of time, or if someone gives us service. Each one of us will pick one or two of the different ways we all feel love. If people around us do not communicate to us using one of the above ways, we'll deem ourselves unlovable. We'll think those around us do not love us and it could be far from the truth. It's important for you to learn and understand yourself.

Am I pretty, handsome, or ugly?

Again, we'll pick what we deem beauty. In some cultures, you're considered beautiful if you're fat, while others view it as the opposite. Sometimes, we'll be teased about being ugly at too young of an age and we'll believe it. If it's our first decision on the subject, we'll find it hard to change.

I discovered that I made a core belief that being old wasn't very beautiful. When I went back, I was two years old. Now, I'm getting closer to being older than younger. I decided to change it. It was interesting how I picked up on it. I felt my feelings change regarding myself and I traced it back to two years old. Our core beliefs are powerful. Before I sent my mind back, I tried using affirmations, but I saw it wasn't working. Then I sent my mind back and discovered that I had made this core belief.

I'm very dumb or smart.

Somehow, I made the decision that I was smart and could figure things out easily. When we first start school, we decide if we like certain subjects and it becomes a core belief. Robert told us that we make a core belief somewhere between first and third grade. He also said that teachers could traumatize us during those first three years and it can affect us for life.

Let me tell you about an experience that shows you how powerful core beliefs can be until they come up against shock. In the first grade, I made a decision that I liked spelling, math, and reading. During the first and second grade, I was in the top reading groups. I always received a hundred percent on spelling and math tests.

In the third grade, I moved to the city with my sister. At my old school, I was taught to read by memorizing my words. In the city, they started the kids out on phonics. The teacher would bring the small group of kids around the blackboard and have them sound out words.

This was a shock for me. The teacher didn't care that I didn't understand how to sound out words. She was old and very impatient. If I didn't sound the words out quickly enough, she would yell at me and even slapped me across the face because of it. I didn't like this teacher and it wasn't helping my situation at home either. Now, you can see why I went into such a deep depression in the third grade and it continued forward. I had no peace at school or home.

I came out of the third grade hating math, reading, and spelling. When I went into the fourth grade, I never could read out loud with ease. My spelling improved, but I didn't always get hundreds on my tests like I used to. I never learned to like math until I met Jack. He loved it and I had him teach me the laws so I could find my enjoyment to do it again.

Can I make friends easily?

Whatever we believe is true will become a reality at a young age. If we've decided making friends is hard at a young age, then we seem to be uncomfortable with it our whole lives. As you can see, we create our own challenges that we have to live with.

I'll be fat or thin when I grow up.

At the age of two, we make a decision by looking at those around us and decide if we'll be thin or heavy. We'll also decide if we love food or if we can take it or leave it. You'll see it within families. Some people will make a core belief that they will be thin or heavy at different ages.

To give you an example, everyone in my family was stick thin. My grandparents were stick thin and my father didn't ever develop a stomach that hung over his belt. So staying thin was easy for me, while in Jack's life it's different.

When we were married, Jack was practically a stick. He stayed that way until he reached a certain age. Suddenly, he put on weight and it happened at the same age his father was when he was two years old. All of his siblings struggle to take and keep weight off.

Lately, they have been talking about children being taught to be heavy on the news by their mothers. I think there is some truth to it and this is how it happens. We base our decisions on what we see in others around us.

The decision to be attracted to the same or opposite sex is a core belief.

This core belief happens around the age of two and no matter how hard we try, it doesn't change by willing it to later in life. Like any core belief, you have to go back to the original decision to change it.

Do I want to love and accept myself?

This is almost self-explanatory. It also happens around the age of two. Most of us decide this from how our caregivers treated us. It also can happen if we find that we're different than others. Some of us have learning handicaps and we need to accept them to live successfully with them.

By default, it usually doesn't happen. It takes others time to realize how frustrating handicaps can be. So it's important that we go back and change it to unconditional love and acceptance. Sometimes, I think people with mental retardation have a good attitude. Some of them have really mastered unconditional love.

You decided that you're inferior to others.

You can make a decision that you're second-rate or inferior to others. Then we blame others for making us feel this way. The truth is you made yourself feel that way by programming your mind that you're inferior. Some people might be better at doing something, but it doesn't mean you're lesser of a person than them.

It's very smart to celebrate other people's gifts and accomplishments. If you choose to be resentful or jealous, then you have just told your mind that you can't have the same thing. Your mind won't allow you to have it. It's very dangerous to covet anything that belongs to someone else. Like it or not, we are programming our minds to keep it away from us.

We all make a decision to what success means to us in our lives.
What has to happen for us to feel success?

Each one of us has placed a standard of living upon ourselves. We usually did it as a core belief so we aren't always consciously aware of it.

If you would go around a crowded room, you would seldom find the same answer to what constitutes the feeling of a successful day.

Some people will put it on money and this isn't smart. You'll go to bed most nights feeling unsuccessful and you could be making a six-digit income. It's important that we feel successful. I heard someone make the rule that they just need to be above ground to feel success. This is great. They'll feel successful by opening their eyes.

If you haven't consciously come up with what makes you feel successful, you can ask your mind to go back to the origin of that decision. By some chance, if you didn't set one up for yourself, do it. Make it as simple as getting out of bed. If you always feel successful, your mind will bring more positive things to you each day.

Am I going to be a happy or an unhappy person?

Believe it or not, we make a core belief if we're going to be happy or unhappy. Some people can go through their whole life and never really be happy. They can't explain why. I made a choice at this age to be happy. After reading about my life, you can see how hard it was for me to be happy. The minute I removed the frozen pictures from my mind, it felt great to be myself again. Basically, I'm a very happy person.

This is something that I would like to share with you. It had an impact on me and I hope you see the point too. One of the first tapes I ever listened to, regarding positive thinking, involved a story about two young boys. One was always happy and the other one was not. In vain, no one could make the one boy happy.

Some researchers wanted to prove that being happy wasn't a choice, but it was instead governed by environment. They picked these two boys from the description of their attitudes. Both boys were placed into rooms with two-way mirrors and speakers, so the researchers could talk with them and give instructions if necessary.

Our unhappy boy was brought into a room filled with the latest toys. Immediately, he ran to the toys, delighted to see all of his choices. The happy boy was named Johnny. He was brought into a room with horse manure in it and nothing else.

When he was left alone, he slowly looked around the whole room. Everyone had their bets on the two boys. Both boys surprised their researchers. Our unhappy boy quickly became frustrated with his toys. He threw them to the ground, crying.

A researcher asked him what his problem was. He picked up each toy and explained what was wrong with it. When he finished with his long explanation of what was wrong with the toys and why he couldn't play with them, some researchers watched Johnny.

Slowly, he started to pick up the horse manure before he chucked it at the wall. As he did it, Johnny started to giggle. Everyone's attention went to Johnny. When the giggling didn't stop, the researchers asked him what he thought was so funny.

He shouted, "With all this manure in here, there has to be a pony somewhere!"

These are our core beliefs that we make as a child. They are easy ones to go back and change, if you know what you're doing. By choosing to be happy, we'll always look at life with eagerness and passion. If you want to live your life like Johnny, I suggest you go back and see what you did and possibly change it. You won't always be happy, but you'll spend most of your time that way.

We decided if we love animals, things, or people as a core belief.

I love animals and people. When I ask my mind to take me back to the time I decided to like animals, I could see it was before I was four years old. In my heart, I know what provoked my decision to love animals. On TV, I was watching Lassie, Fury, Roy Roger's Trigger, and Rin Tin Tin. They were heroes of the animal kingdom and I decided that I wanted an animal hero.

Jack can take or leave animals. He doesn't dislike them, but he never made a decision to fall in love with them. He really doesn't have an opinion, but he does love my animals. When I asked him to go back and find out why, I learned he never saw the value of them like I did. Some of us need to be loved with a lick on the face. Animals are therapeutic for us and Jack has changed his core belief.

How you handle stress and negative experiences is a core belief.

This one basically comes down to two choices. We make a decision that it's important to hold stress and negative experiences, along with their emotions, inside of us. I mentioned earlier in the book that exercise helps to relieve stress. It's the deep breathing that releases it. Under stress, we tighten up and so does our breathing.

Make sure your core beliefs are that you let stress and negative emotions pass through you. It's a common choice that children will hold onto the negative. Then we carry it around with us. I like to describe it as a stick that we drag behind us, so we can hit ourselves with it when we do something that we're not pleased with.

Are we going to be a honest person or not?

Believe it or not, we'll make these decisions before the age of two. We will choose if it's important to be honest or not. Some people will make the choice that it isn't very important to be honest.

As I was writing this book, I saw something interesting on the news. They showed a surveillance camera in a store and the person behind the counter was called away. A woman and her two-year-old daughter were standing close by the counter, looking at the items on the shelves.

When the clerk left, the young mother ran behind the counter with her daughter following her. The young mother was rifling through the clerk's purse.

Immediately, when the two-year-old saw her mother, she ran out from behind the counter and headed to the shelves. She started to pull things off. Her mother saw her little girl and said, "Honey, leave those things there. They aren't yours and you shouldn't take them."

I shook my head and said to myself, "That little girl isn't stupid. She knows what her mother was doing. The little girl knows what her mother's purse looks like and she was aware that her mother was in someone else's." Our actions have far more power with our children than our words. They did arrest the woman.

We choose love or hate as a foundation of our lives.

Every thought, every action, and every word we deliver is with love or hate. People will feel it before they hear our words. Our spirits respond to the love, while hate pushes others away. Remember, any negative thought translates into the emotion of hate.

Let me share an example with you on how our spirits respond to love. I happen to have twin grandsons. At a young age, they can become the same as a pack of dogs. The boys happened to be six and they were staying at my house, while their parents were building their new home.

On the first day, they took a bath in my jetted tub. Of course, they wanted the jets on and I obliged. Before they entered the tub, Grandma left them with instructions on what was acceptable behavior and what wasn't. I forgot one of the instructions, since I didn't understand it was possible.

One of the boys pointed the jets at the ceiling. For some reason, I didn't think about that one. Later, I entered the bathroom to be greeted by a man-made rainstorm. Immediately, the joy on their faces disappeared after seeing Grandma. It only took me minutes to realize how much fun they were having.

In a low, loving, but firm voice, I informed, "Boys, this doesn't make me happy. You're ruining my things. I can see you're having a lot of fun, but I never want to see this again. Do we understand each other?"

They responded back with a yes and quickly turned off the jets. Afterwards, they exited the tub, grabbing a towel to wrap around their waists. Without being asked, they joined me in cleaning up the bathroom. We did it together and they seemed nervous about what I was going to do to them.

When we finished, I thanked them for helping me before I left. When they exited the bathroom, one of the twins put his arms around my waist and peered up at me. "Grandma, thank you for not yelling at us."

Smiling, I answered, "You mean more to me than my bathroom. Will you promise to respect my things and not do it again?"

"Yes," they both answered.

So far, this was the last time I had this conversation with the boys. Their spirits responded to my love first so they could hear my words. You can tell anyone anything with success if they know that you love them. My grandsons knew that I loved them more than I did my things. This builds their self-worth and love and this is important.

Now, did I do that with my children? Probably not.. However, if they had spilt milk, I didn't yell at them. I wanted my kids to know that they were more important than the milk.

When I had children, I didn't have all the knowledge that I have today. So I did just like everyone else and made numerous mistakes. They were definitely my mistakes and not my ancestors'. It felt wonderful to not pass them on to my children. Did I disappoint or hurt them? Oh, yes. Did they disappoint me? Not really. I admire how they deal with their challenges and trials and I hope they embrace them. Mother still doesn't know very much, so they don't want to hear from me.

We decide on the kind of person we'll marry.

From my research, we choose what kind of a personality we're drawn to before the age of five. You can choose them on an unconscious level. For an example, if Harold, Jen, and Mary hated what our father did to them, then they'll marry someone like him, instead of someone with Mother's kind, loving ways.

Hate plays a stronger role and the mind doesn't understand the difference between hate or love. Bud and I weren't with our father long enough to make that choice to hate the way he treated us. We fell in love with our grandfather. He would play with us while Grandmother kept her distance when he was around. We both picked someone like him. My grandmother's abusive behavior only cemented my attachment towards him.

People can change. It took Mary's spouse until he was in his sixties to change. He treats her with a lot of kindness today. I see his love for her in his eyes. It wasn't there in the early days. However, as for Harold and Jen, I still see the same behavior in their spouses by the way they treat others.

Will we be a hard worker or lazy?

This is one of the very first decisions that we make. Another person cannot determine if someone is a hard worker or not. We can make the decision, but it won't kick in until we choose it to. Sometimes, we chose to work hard if it's something that we love. Other people made a decision to work hard on every task that's given to them. Then we have others who want to take the easy road. Little do they know that they'll work harder on the easy road than if they just chose to be a hard worker. They also miss what hard work does for you. It builds self-worth, love, and character.

We created who we are today by our choices. By changing your choices, you create a new person. There are numerous core beliefs that we pick in the beginning of our lives. I just put together some that you might identify with, so you can go back and change some of them if you want. It's a great feeling to take back your life and create the kind of person you want to be.

How do you change core beliefs that you decided on as a child?

If you want to change a core belief, mentally ask your mind to go back to the origin of a decision. When you arrive at the age you made the decision, then remove the old decision. Here is a suggestion for you: I would take out a small box from my pocket and place the old decision in it.

Then bring out a balloon from your pocket and fill it with helium gas. Next, I would tie the box with my old decision onto the balloon. Then I would let the balloon go and watch it disappear. When it has disappeared, then I would make a new decision. It helps to express it out loud.

After doing this, then ask your mind to take you back to the present with your new decision. Once in the present, send the decision into the future indefinitely throughout the eternities. If you've done it right, you should feel a deep sigh.

I would like to summarize what we have learned in this chapter. Core beliefs are very powerful and they can and do control our lives with an iron fist. Now, I hope you feel comfortable with being able to change them and start to create the kind of person you want to be. You need to change the core belief because you can't will it to change in the future.

In the next chapter, we're going to be talking about the laws that govern true happiness. There are certain rules that we need to follow if we want to be happy even when everything around us is falling apart.

Chapter 17

Laws That Govern Happiness

What is happiness? Where does it come from? Some of us humans think if we had everything now that we ever wanted, then we would be happy. It will never happen. You need to make the choice first to be happy. You do not want to anchor happiness to a thing, person, or an event. As children, we happen to make this mistake.

The reason why we shouldn't anchor happiness to these things is because we'll never feel happiness without choosing to feel it first. Besides, people, things, and events are fleeting. Do you really want your happiness in someone else's control?

Life is a journey, not a destination. It's always evolving and sometimes our lives go into directions that we really don't want. If you're happy to begin with, you'll learn a lot from the different directions that you go into. It's important to appreciate your life.

What is the first and most important rule of happiness?

When I was fourteen, someone I dearly respected told me to love my trials. They are what make you, you. This whole statement upset me when I heard it and I became angry. How dare they tell me to love my trials! Do they really understand what I went through? At the time, I was still reliving the nightmare each day of my life.

Finally, I decided to love my trials and it was the most fantastic thing I ever did. When we love our trials, we love ourselves. By loving us, it brings great joy in a way that's hard to describe. Sometimes, we go through some really tough trials. No matter what happens to us, we come out of it fine. We aren't really hurt. It's only how our minds view it as a damaging experience. Then it will affect us.

How should we treat our trials?

1. Trials are usually painful and uncomfortable. Some of them even scar us in ways we can't see, as we have talked about in this book. When we love our trials, the love neutralizes the pain and can melt the shock as we mentally put our arms around ourselves.
2. By loving your trials, you're able to understand the values and lessons that are in them. By loving them, you can use the tragedy as a strong foundation to build your life upon.
3. The love for the trial will stop your mind from causing you to repeat it. By truly loving your trials, you will elevate yourself to a higher level of understanding and vision. This is valuable.

When I was back at the farm, I mentioned sitting on the hillside, watching the hawks fly high overhead. I so wished that I could have had the ability to see the valley though a hawk's perspective. They would be able to see the whole valley at once and understand so much of what was going on.

Looking away from the sky, I could lower my vision to see the ants scouring around the gravel on the hillside. The ants had no concept of my vision of their surroundings or the hawks'. They probably didn't even see me watching them.

Sometimes, we get trapped in the thinking of an ant. We can become so focused on our daily chores that we become unaware of the other things going on around us. Therefore, we miss wonderful opportunities. Some of us scurry around, not wanting to face our lives and the complete picture of what we can become.

Many times, there are wonderful opportunities attached to our trials. If we are all caught up in being angry, bitter, or discouraged, we don't see the possibilities. Plus, we keep bringing towards us what we don't want to have happen.

How do we keep ourselves happy?

I've mentioned before that the most important rule of becoming happy is being grateful for your trials and your life. It really is the surest way to bring good and wonderful things towards you while you enjoy the process. Deciding to go through life being happy is far superior than viewing everything in life negatively.

I found being negative to be very painful and it attracted the same kind of people into my life. When people are negative and unhappy, they can also be abusive. It's the byproduct of being in a negative thought-pattern.

You might find this strange, but the best rule of conduct on being happy I've seen is the Alcoholics Anonymous pledge. Since my biggest challenge in life is my thoughts, I've been so long into negative thoughts that I treated myself like an alcoholic. It would mean a lot to share with you their creed and why it's really a good standard to follow if you want to be happy.

The other reason I found it good is that I've yet to meet someone who hasn't been addicted to some kind of chemical. With me, it was the negative thoughts I had about my life and myself. It was destroying my health and happiness and I was constantly bringing moments I didn't want in my life.

This is their pledge and I like it for a standard of living my life.

Here are the twelve steps of Alcoholics Anonymous:
1. We admitted we were powerless over alcohol-that our lives had become unmanageable.
2. Came to believe that a Power greater than ourselves could restore us to sanity.
3. Made a decision to turn our will and our lives over to the care of God as we understood Him.
4. Made a searching and fearless moral inventory of ourselves.
5. Admitted to God, to ourselves, and to another human being the exact nature of our wrongs.

6. Were entirely ready to have God remove all these defects of character.
7. Humbly asked Him to remove our shortcomings.
8. Made a list of all persons we had harmed, and became willing to make amends to them all.
9. Made direct amends to such people wherever possible, except when to do so would injure them or others.
10. Continued to take personal inventory and when we were wrong promptly admitted it.
11. Sought through prayer and meditation to improve our conscious contact with God, as we understood Him, praying only for knowledge of His will for us and the power to carry that out.
12. Having had a spiritual awakening as the result of these steps, we tried to carry this message to alcoholics, and to practice these principles in all our affairs.

Alcoholics Anonymous World Services, Inc.

By living this motto, we keep the spirit in control. With our spirits in charge, we're happier and we can handle our trials with success. What is another way to discover our true selves?

Meditation is wonderful. It helps you to get in touch with your spirit. I like to take a subject and meditate on it. This is how I learn all the different aspects of happiness. It's a good time to look at it from every angle and when you do, you learn about what you want to understand from your life.

The steps below are what I have meditated upon so I could understand them more. I would like to share them with you. If you'll follow every step to the fullest, you'll find the kind of happiness that shines in your face. It's coming from your soul out.

Step one: Honesty

This is so simple and yet so powerful. Being honest can bring so many wonderful things into your life. When you are honest in all things, you are thinking positively about your life and you. So you're bringing wonderful events and people into your life.

Honesty is also based on love while dishonesty is based on hate. Dishonesty is deliberately hurting others. So you really have to dislike yourself to hurt someone else on purpose. It's impossible to be dishonest and be happy.

The first person you want to be honest with is yourself. This next statement, I want you to remember. If you'll lie to yourself, then you'll lie to someone else. If you make a rule to never lie to yourself, then you won't lie to someone else. Some people decided to become addicted to lying. If they had a rule to never lie to themselves, then they wouldn't have gotten started with it. Usually, they made the decision to become addicted by hating the fact that someone lied to them and they won't let it go.

When you are honest in all areas of your life, you respect yourself and so will others. I always appreciated the stories about President Abraham Lincoln. What an honor to have the name Honest Abe. In one word, it expresses his life and who he was.

Step two: Hope

Hope is the positive and it's a form of faith. This is very important. Like I have mentioned before, without hope we become depressed. I think hope is the hardest thought to live without. I'm so grateful it's a choice that no one can take away from me.

When you have hope in every aspect of your life, you are bringing love towards you and your spirit needs it to be healthy. It will build your love, self-confidence, and self-esteem. It's a very powerful healer.

One of my first dreams was just to have hope. I found it to be soothing towards my broken self and it was very healing. I'm so grateful for hope and how it affects our lives. It's a very positive emotion and it has a powerful impact on our lives. Without it, we couldn't have taken our first breath of air.

Step three: Trust in Your God

I didn't heal on my own. When I turned my life over to Him as a child, my burdens became lighter and bearable. It was He who showed me how thick my frozen moments of shock were inside of me. He kept sending me back when I would die or beg to die. He showed me how to walk out of darkness and into the light. So I know no other way but to love God with all my heart.

Some of us do not have the same God. Yet, every human has to have a God. It's our nature. What is the dearest thing to you? You'll find it right next to your heart. It can be a thing, an idea, an emotion, or a person. Whatever comes to your mind when you ask the question is your God.

If you're not sure, I suggest you look at yourself and say, "Mind, show me what is the most dearest thing to me in my heart." Some of us will find the love of power, things, addictions, or principles as their Gods. What do you have next to your heart?

Step four: Truth

I love truth. Why? It's very powerful and truth has never let me down. Remember my friend in the eighth grade, who lied about me so she could get what she wanted? It didn't hurt me, but it did hurt her. When the truth comes out, and I promise you, it will let everyone know what really happened. My friend was exposed as a liar and lost respect from others and herself.

To me, truth is a shield that will always protect you. If you have the right attitude, the truth will edify you to a higher plane of understanding and joy. Stay close to the truth in all things and it will never let you down.

Step five: Confession

If you've made a mistake, admit to it as fast as you can. It frees you and it protects your self-love and worth. You'll have respect for yourself by admitting it. We all make mistakes, so why do you want to hide them? If you're telling yourself that you need to be perfect, then what is perfection? Every person out there has a different opinion of what it is. You'll find trying to achieve perfection is like trying to thread a needle blindfolded. It can't be done. Confessing to making a mistake keeps you from lying to yourself. This is a trap that you don't want to be caught in.

I suggest you do what Kathy did, my friend who came back and told the truth about what happened to me in the eighth grade. If you can't tell the truth to the person you hurt, then you might want to find someone within your religion. Sometimes, it isn't smart to tell your friends if it's going to burden them. Sometimes, you only need to confess to yourself or your creator. I like to do it in prayer unless it is something major and I've really hurt someone else.

Step six: Change of Heart

This means you've made a decision to change your life. If you've decided to change, then you must start with your thoughts. So now, your feelings are going to change, which means the future will be different for you.

I love the quote from Winston Churchill. It sat on my desk while I was learning to write. It says, "To improve is to change; to be perfect is to change often." Every time I felt discouraged, I would look at the saying, take a deep breath, and try to learn my way out of my situation.

Step seven: Humility

I would not be writing books if I didn't have a passion for this virtue. Humility has opened numerous doors to me. It is very important and I really want to impress this upon your mind. It's impossible to change, heal, or learn something new without humility.

Negative thoughts and humility can't survive together. One has to win out and I think it should be humility. It's a thought that is based totally on love and it can take you anywhere you want. You're open to learning the secrets that will teach you how to accomplish what you want.

Step eight: Seek Forgiveness

If you've offended others, it's very smart to ask them to forgive you. It is extremely important to forgive yourself for being a victim or making a mistake. By forgiving, you're releasing any negative thoughts and emotions that you had. Asking forgiveness frees you, so you can go on with your new thoughts. This includes you asking to forgive yourself. You can't make a change or heal without doing it.

Step nine: Restitution and Reconciliation

If you made mistakes big enough to really hurt someone, then you need to make restitution to them. It will rebuild your self-love and respect. You can walk away from the situation feeling good about yourself. It's also a chance to keep a friend for a lifetime.

Step ten: Daily Accountability

This is important to each one of us. I think this is why I liked to write my feelings in a journal. It's a way to make accountability to myself so I'm not falling back into a trap. My trap is negative thinking. Another place I like to report into is during my nightly prayers. It feels good to talk about what excited or confused me, or what I needed. When I do this, it keeps me from feeling lonely. This is a big negative emotion that I have to deal with. I'm so grateful for prayer and I believe very strongly in it.

Step eleven: Personal Guidance

I bet you're wondering why I put this in the book. Like I said earlier, I feel there is a path for each one of us to follow. If we find it, then the reward is happiness. To find the path, I like to pray and then meditate. It's a time for you to find an alignment with your spirit, your creator, and what you want to accomplish.

The place I learned this was after I watched a movie on Gandhi's life. He meditated on a regular basis and I find it to be extremely helpful. I've heard other people mention the same thing. If you haven't tried it, then I suggest you do.

Step twelve: Service

I saved the best for last. It hurt so much to not be able to give a Mother's Day present to someone, when we were asked to make it at school. It did remove the sting of my pain to give or do service for someone who didn't expect it. When you give service with love, it comes back to you in boatloads. I can perfectly understand why Mother Teresa worked so hard to give service. She probably died happier than most of us could ever imagine.

To give another example, I love the story of *Les Miserables* by Victor Hugo. When the bishop in the Catholic Church had his silver stolen by Jean Valjean, the ex-con, he gave the silver to him. When the police bring him and the silver back, the bishop understood the laws of giving to others. He gives the silver to Jean Valjean and he becomes a man of honor and respect.

The key to service is to give without expecting anything back. You give solely out of love. Some people have been forced to give service to a community as their punishment. It pleases me to see, in some people, their heart soften and they start to understand how wonderful it feels to give service.

Embrace and accept your future and accept anything it brings into your life.

This is a statement of faith. So often, we are afraid of the unknown. We are afraid of the future because we aren't sure what is coming. Maybe, we might not be able to handle the future. The truth is we can handle it. You have handled everything so far. You will be okay.

You might always want to remember that change is good. We should be grateful for it. The future will always bring change. We can always count on it, just like death and taxes. By you being grateful every day for change, you can appreciate everything that is going on within your life.

It's so wonderful to live without being afraid of the unknown. This is one that I wished I would've figured out years ago. It never happened until I melted my moments of shock and paid attention to my feelings.

Learn what you love to do and do it.

For years, I was a person who felt like there was nothing special about me. So I really never felt excited to get out of bed to do something that I wanted to do. Like I told you before, I got sick and found my love for writing.

When you do what you love, you'll find yourself healthy and your quality of life improves. I've never been so happy as I am today, writing.

My love was so impaired for so many years. However, I'm enjoying my time now. The phrase, "When one door closes for you, another one will open," is so true with me.

**Stop yourself from feeling overwhelmed, negative, or lashing out at others.
Be patient with yourself and you'll be patient with others.**

The above emotions take away our happiness. We are afraid that we might not be able to handle the opportunities that are at our doorsteps. Sometimes, we push opportunities away because we allow ourselves to feel overwhelmed.

When you feel it, you need to tell yourself that you can do it. Each day, you'll figure it out and you'll be okay. If we aren't moving our thoughts away from the negative, we will lash out at others. When they approach us to do one more thing, we feel like our plates are already too full. A busy person is the one who gets things done. I marvel as I learn to handle the different events on my plate.

Stop worrying about what people think about you.

We all want to be accepted. It's a basic human need. Most of us want and expect others to give it to us. If we do this, then we are in trouble. It really needs to come from you. You need to unconditionally accept yourself.

If you don't, you might do dumb things just to please others. In the second grade, the class read a story that has never left my thoughts. I would like to share it with you so you can decide for yourself.

As I remember, the story started off with a father and son leaving their home with a donkey. It was morning and they were taking the donkey to the market to sell it. The family needed the money more than the donkey. To get to the market, the father and son had to pass through various towns.

At the first town, some people asked them where they were going. When they told them, one person said, "That's a long way to be walking today. Why aren't you allowing your son to ride your donkey? He's so young."

The father became embarrassed and placed his son on the back of the donkey before they left the town. At the next town, the son was still riding the donkey. The same thing happened in this town.

When people asked the father where they were going, he told them. Someone said, "Oh that's a long way to go. Boy, you should get off the donkey and let your father ride him. You're younger than he is. He's older and desires to ride." Again, the two looked at each other and decided to trade before leaving the town.

When they entered the next town, people were pointing and making fun of them. They said, "You have a donkey and you both aren't riding him." The father put out his hand so his son could join him. Together, they rode the donkey to the next town. This is where they were going to sell him.

It was getting dark and they needed to hurry, so their buyer wouldn't leave. They urged the donkey faster, only to have him collapse at the edge of town. The father and son were stunned to realize their donkey was dead. Now, they had nothing to sell and they needed the money. Disappointed, they had to pay to remove the body of the donkey and went home without any money and with nothing else to sell.

Thinking about each town's point of view, I thought they all had valid points of view. They didn't understand what the father and son were trying to accomplish. It taught me a lesson that people's opinions are usually narrow and limited because they can't see everything that you're trying to accomplish. So you shouldn't expect people to tell you what to do. This is your decision.

What are the basic rules or laws of happiness?

I want to summarize what we have talked about in this chapter. People, things, and events do not make us happy. It's dangerous to think things and people can make you happy. Yet, so many times we've bought into this theory. Some people will place their happiness on an event. We aren't aware that we have programmed our minds to think this way. How many times have you said you'll be happy when someone or something is here or done?

The basic rules I outlined really do bring true happiness. When we love ourselves, we are truly happy and it shows in our faces. It might sound very silly to say honesty, gratefulness, compassion, or giving service are what brings you joy. They might be outdated and old-fashion, but they are powerful and can transform your life.

When you get at the end of your life and look back, you might see they are what keeps and brings joy into your life. I can testify to you from personal experience that they do affect your life in a very positive way. I've been on both sides of the street. The statement, "options on all things," is very true.

As miserable as my life was in the beginning, the joy today matches it. I look forward to the future, not being afraid anymore. This is wonderful. In the next chapter, I want to talk about separation from the ones we love. As you already know, I have a lot of experience with it.

Chapter 18

How to Handle Separation

This subject is one we all would like to avoid. There is no one in this life that hasn't faced it at least once. We all push it away, hoping it won't come into our lives. However, it does and there is really nothing we can do to stop it from happening. Separation can be very valuable in our lives. There are some very important lessons that we can learn from it. You never appreciate it until it happens and you have some hindsight to go along with it.

In my life, I had experienced eight different separations by the time I was thirty. They all felt the same and there is a pattern of healing that you need to go through. In my opinion, the hardest separations are the ones where people don't die. With a death, you at least have closure. When people split through divorce, they still have to see each other. This is what happened to my grandmother. What hurt her the most was she never had the opportunity to really know her father. Her parents divorced soon after her birth.

A divorce can continue to have old wounds open up and keep hurting. This is the one that I want to focus on the most. I cannot say I've been through a divorce. However, the feelings are the same when living in a home without actually being part of the family. When you leave the home, the door is always shut for you.

The hardest time in your life is when you realize that you can't go back or you aren't welcomed at a place you have spent your life at. Bud, Mary, and I have experienced this feeling. None of us were welcomed back to a place where we only knew as home. During the holidays, when families gather together, we never had a place to go home to.

In our state, the foster programs are adopting children out instead of finding them a temporary home to live and I applaud them. In my case, I was told where I lived wasn't my home, but emotionally you need to feel like you belong somewhere. I've often wondered what it would be like to go back to a place where you have memories or even be invited to a family event and be included.

So how do you handle it?

A separation from a death or divorce is really treated the same. Divorce is harder because you can still see those people and they let you know that you're not a part of their lives by their actions. So this is what you do:

Embrace the fact that you're separated.

In my case, I was in an abusive situation. What I hungered for weren't people, but the hopes of being loved and welcomed as a part of a family. This is what kids and adults go through with a divorce. They hunger for a loving relationship and it hurts to wake up one day and realize your dreams and hopes are shattered.

In some divorces, you feel betrayed and I felt that from Jen. I trusted her and she tricked me into living with her and her family only so they could use me. The same can be said in a bad marriage. Never should you expect to change a person. This is a huge falsehood. We can only change ourselves. If you are in a bad relationship, then you need to make some decisions for yourself.

You might want to mentally put your arms around yourself and say that it's okay. It's okay that you made decisions that brought so much pain and sorrow into your life. If the pain isn't recent, then I suggest you go back to your younger self and put your arms around her or him and say, "I'm from the future and I want you to know that you'll be okay. This experience is going to give you character, so embrace it with love."

Once your younger self feels the love, you should ask your mind to bring that love to the present and take it off into the future. If you're doing this, you'll start to feel the pain leave you.

This is only a start. There are other steps.

Step two: Anger

The next stage of separation is anger. You'll become angry after you realize what really happened. When I got away from my sister, I was very angry that she was so selfish. I was also angry that my mother and father had left me feeling no hope or security. My grandmother had also let me down. All I wanted was to be loved and accepted. Was I asking too much?

No, I wasn't and it's important that you let out all of your anger. Some people never come out of this stage and it can be dangerous for your health. I know this to be true because I ruined my immune system with my anger and fears of life.

I carried it for decades and it stole my happiness and I attracted other people into my life who were angry too and it didn't help me.

Today, I give myself a set of minutes or hours to feel my anger. Then I tell my mind to dump the anger. It's interesting to have the anger leave after the set time I give my mind. **You want to rid yourself of the anger quickly.**

What comes after anger?

Understanding! Sometimes, we want this before we let go of our anger. It's impossible to see any understanding, when you're in the anger stage. Some people never allow themselves to come out of the anger stage. We all need to look back and see what really happened. What role did I play in the separation? Sometimes, you made mistakes and other times you picked the wrong person for you.

With understanding, is the separation better or worse for you? The answer lies in how you chose to handle it. If you truly have given up your anger, you'll see the lessons and benefits that the change has on your life. In my case, it was better for me to be divorced from so much abuse than to be a part of my sister's family.

By taking the lesson I learned, I became stronger and wiser. It gave me the ability to choose wisely, knowing the damage someone can cause in others' lives by being selfish and abusive. We all have the ability to choose what we want in life and we should never expect others to make choices for us.

Some people chose to be easily offended and this is also very dangerous. If you chose to be easily offended by others, then it means you're selfish and you do not love yourself.

Any kind of separation becomes a part of you, so love it. When you do, it will edify you to a higher level of understanding, self-love, and respect from others besides yourself. Everything in your life becomes a part of you, so it's so important to love your trials. If you want to keep your self-love and worth, remember no one can give it to you but you.

What is the next step?

Let it go! It's okay it happened. You came out of it being a better person. When you choose to have the right attitudes, your trials enhance you and they make you a better, wiser person. You need to tell yourself it's okay and that you learned a lot.

The last step.

Forgive! You need to forgive everyone involved in the separation, including yourself. You really need to put your arms around yourself and ask forgiveness for bringing so much pain into your life. This is the most healing you can do.

A lot of times, we'll forgive everyone but ourselves. Then we wonder why we aren't receiving the peace that forgiving should give us. It's forgiving yourself that gives you the peace you seek.

You probably have questions. I'm going to try and anticipate some of them for you. There are only a few and I hope to have picked the right ones.

What if I find myself wanting to blame someone else for the separation? Does blaming cause me problems?

Yes, it does. When you blame, you're not willing to heal and move on with your life. It also means you're not ready to face yourself and deal with the pain. The pain will never go away until you face it. With time, the pain will only get worse. It's okay to feel the pain and anger, if you'll work through it and let it go.

Stop with the blame. It will stop you from moving on with your life and healing. If you have children, you aren't setting a good example. You are teaching them how to stay trapped in negative emotions. They are looking at you to show them how to handle the situation.

So be careful what you say about the other person. Sometimes, we want to lash out at others. What you say about others will become a part of you. This is something that you might want to talk with your kids about. They are feeling the same as you even if they are adults. You might want to tell them that it's normal to feel pain, anger, and betrayal. They are normal feelings in this situation. They will follow your example because they are in a situation that they aren't familiar with. Kids have a tendency to take the responsibility of a separation upon themselves.

I admire people who handle it right with divorce or death. They don't whine about their situation because of it. People are attracted to them. You can help others in your family who are suffering just by finding peace. It should give them hope.

The steps you need to go through are the same for death and divorce. If you haven't found peace with divorce, you can reopen wounds or never allow yourself to heal and learn from it. One advantage of death is you can remember your loved ones the way you want to. In life, I've found Jen to come back like a bad dream. With me being healed, I can genuinely smile at her and feel sorry for the pain she keeps inflicting upon herself. She can't touch me, since I'm a whole person and not fractured. It's a wonderful place to learn your way into. It's my choice if I ever allow someone else to really hurt me.

To summarize what we talked about, I want to quickly repeat the steps of how to handle separation.

1. Embrace the fact that it happened and like the Alcoholics Anonymous motto, it is out of your control. It's okay to acknowledge that it happened. Some people think if they don't recognize it, the pain will just melt away and it doesn't.

2. Let the anger out. It's normal and expected. Please, you need to allow it to go away as quickly as you can. It isn't healthy to allow it to stay.

3. You'll want to satisfy yourself with understanding why and what happened. Please, you need to remember that we must leave blame out of the equation. Blame blinds you from seeing the truth and here it is important.

4. Let it go! You need to allow all the positive and negative emotions to go away. Love the experience for how it has changed your life. When you love it, you are giving love to yourself. The experience is now a part of you, so let your spirit know that it's okay.

5. Forgive everyone who was a part of the separation and especially yourself. Kids need to learn how to forgive themselves for being in a family that split up. Otherwise, they blame themselves and this is what we want to avoid.

These are the five steps that will help you get through a separation. So many times, people take their pain into a new relationship. After a while, it affects this relationship too.

You should heal before you go into another one. If you keep experiencing a bad situation, it can't help but hurt your self-esteem and love. Remember, if you don't love yourself, then you have a hard time feeling other people's love. You might not know it because you have nothing to compare your life against.

I want to add one more thing. Sometimes, separation can be felt because someone is a victim of a violent crime and they lived to tell the story. The steps apply here. It's very important that you go back and just hold yourself. Then assure yourself that you are going to be okay so you can melt the shock. Then the steps above will work very well for you.

In the next chapter, I want to summarize the whole book. Join me for one last chapter.

Chapter 19

Mastering the White Paper

I hope as you read my story, you could see how good or abusive habits are passed on from one generation to another. We keep passing them on unless we do something about healing ourselves. When you take the step to heal and stop the abuse, it frees you and your progeny from being trapped in old repeated behaviors.

Our ancestors came from a hard life. Without the knowledge that we know today, they made numerous mistakes. For an example, it was cruel for the medical field not to tell my mother that she was dying of a fast and deadly cancer. Most of the behaviors we have are taught. All the behaviors start with a thought or decision.

You can stop the past from repeating itself and start to build your own life. Now, you can remove the moments of shock, pain, fear, and disappointment. You can dictate what you want to happen in your own life and live it with passion. It's yours, so own it with open arms of love.

Now, you have the keys to unlock your cage. What are you going to write on your white paper of life? What do you want to accomplish now that you have the freedom to do something? This is always a question that I ask myself. What else am I going to learn or understand, regarding myself?

It's exciting to discover a new talent or gift that I didn't know existed inside of me because of the negative thoughts and emotions. With my crippling fear gone, I'm looking forward to seeing how my life will evolve. You have so many choices and it's okay to have them.

You'll make the right decision and if you find one that wasn't the best, embrace it. That way, you can learn a lot from the wrong decision so you'll know what direction you're going into. When Thomas Edison's early experiments with the light bulb went nowhere, instead of giving up, he said he learned several thousand ways it wouldn't work.

I have a powerful testimony of **prayer**. It started when I reached out while being at my lowest points. My first prayer was answered with the warm invisible arms surrounding me. I felt like I would be saved as long as I didn't offend Him. Yes, I've been made fun of by others because I put so much faith in Him. They just haven't walked in my shoes and seen all of the miracles that flow into my life. Prayer has and will always be the cornerstone of my life.

Some people tell me they are frustrated with their answers and that they can't get answers from prayers. Yes you can. The secret to getting a prayer answered is to approach it as a little child would. A child wouldn't have negative thoughts. When my mother died, I prayed with total faith that I would be answered.

The secret is to not have any hidden agenda. Too many times, we pray and ask for something to happen. We picture in our minds exactly what we want to have happen, while we ask.

With my first prayer, I pictured nothing. I reached for help and was willing to accept any answer. This is the secret of prayer: to reach out from the depths of your heart without any agenda. As a child does from their parents, you accept any answer.

A lot of times, we feel frustrated with prayer because we approach it with an attitude of daring Him to give us what we ask for. Some people approach prayer with the thought that they will only accept His answer if He answered a certain way only. You have tied His hands to give it to you. There is no humility. You also tie His hands with negative thoughts. He cannot tolerate them, so we stop Him from being able to reach us.

You control the situation by the environment you've created around yourself. You need to be in a positive state of mind to receive answers and build a relationship. He is always there. You block Him by your thoughts. I'm testifying to you that He cannot reach you as long as you are negative in your thoughts.

If you have the right attitude, He will answer your prayers. We all know a child is humble so they can learn. This is why humility is so important. Our answers might not come the second we ask. Instead, people will come into our lives and happen to say something. If you are humble and sincerely waiting for your answer, you'll find it instantly. What they just said is your answer. You'll know by the warm feeling in your chest area. Some people have been receiving them their whole lives, but didn't know what the burning sensation meant.

In reading about a new concept, you aren't sure about it. I suggest you pray and ask for further knowledge. I promise, you'll be answered if you're patient and humble like a little child.

There's another thing I suggest you do. I've mentioned before you might want to keep a journal, regarding your feelings. That way, you can understand what kind of thoughts you are having. I would write down what you learned. Sometimes, we forget about principles that worked very well for us. We move on and suddenly things stop working for us.

It's called going back to the basics. If you haven't written down what you learned and how it helped your life, then the mind can easily get distracted and you need to have it stay focused. It's okay to have more than one journal.

Since I'm talking about writing in a journal, some people are in a situation of taking care of a family member with dementia or another personality-changing disease. You need to add another step. First, you need to know that you're handling a very lonely and touchy situation. It hurts to see someone who was a strength to you revert into a little child mentally.

To help, I suggest you take a piece of paper and write down all of your frustrations. Write as fast as you can and do not worry about periods, spelling, or the structure of your sentences. You need to pour out your frustrations upon the paper. Now, this is important. I'm going to ask you to not read what you wrote. You'll reenter the information into your mind if you read it.

When you feel like you have dumped everything on the paper, you need to put your pen down and pick up the paper. I want you to rip it up and throw it into the garbage. This will help you cope with the frustration of helping someone you love who has stopped recognizing you.

Sometimes, we also get frustrated with how slowly things are happening in our lives. Dreams are precious and we need to cherish them. So often, we are quick to hide or quit on them. It's our dreams that give us passion to live a full life and enjoy ourselves. If they are big, some just take time, like my dream to have a horse.

Be patient with yourself. You'll figure something out if you never give up. Sometimes, it takes a while for the information to reach us, but it comes. I'm so grateful I didn't give up on healing from my past. It took me twenty-five years of learning other principles until I learned how the mind handles shock and other emotions. I didn't quit and it could've been so easy.

I'm grateful someone crossed my path and told me to love my trials. It freed me from an invisible cage that I wasn't happy being in and didn't know it. I'm grateful to have experience in my life. At times, I felt like I was swimming in a deep dark ocean alone.

I'm grateful for learning the power of unconditional love and I give it to myself. If someone else feels it from me, they are feeling it because I have something to share. You can't give what you don't have for yourself. Unconditional love is a wonderful feeling and I'm grateful I understand how to give it to myself, so I'm not waiting for someone else to give it to me.

One important principle to remember:

You can stop yourself from achieving your goal by forcing it to happen faster than it's ready to. Force is seldom good for us. If we force something to happen in our lives, it will take our dreams twice as long to come to us.

I love history and I've never seen how force has helped any group of people. Some people like to force their beliefs on others. We all need and deserve to have the opportunity to choose our own dreams. Without choosing, we lose the passion to live our lives to the fullest.

Again, if you're working on a large goal or dream, you need to remind yourself that it might take time. In the meantime, you can learn and build confidence by working on smaller goals. I promise it will happen if you aren't causing your mind to stop bringing what you want towards you.

Dream big enough so you can become passionate about it.

To be happy, it's important you find something that you can be passionate about. It's the passion that makes the journey in your life rewarding. If you haven't become passionate about something in your life, then you've missed something. Passion is a positive emotion. It's important for you to bring your mind, spirit, body, and emotions together so you can achieve your dream. Passion brings everyone together and it helps you to be in harmony for it to happen.

Most dreams involve more people than just you. Do not be afraid to dream big. People like to become involved with dreams that are big enough for them to participate in. You might have just ignited something within them.

Decide to enjoy your life.

This is a reminder of how important our choices are in our lives. You can become anything you want. You will find your greatest joy if you find the path that is meant for you. I believe before I came into this existence, there was a path for me to follow. What I needed to do was choose to follow it.

I also have a strong testimony that choice is given to every living cell. After I received an answer that every living cell has a choice, I pondered about my life. Why did I choose a hard life? In my heart, I wouldn't be surprised if I wanted to learn my way out so I could understand the laws of true success. I must have known that you needed to touch a hot pan to understand that you do not want to touch a hot pan. Little did I know how painful my path would become for me.

The rewards will come to us if we find that path and live it with passion. I'm very grateful for my past and what I went through. There is nothing that I fear now. Why should I be afraid? I've already experienced every emotion and lived. I'm okay and the pain has been healed with His help. The same will happen to you.

I hope you make the choice to enjoy your journey so you can discover your true self. I love watching people achieve their goals. I'm looking forward to seeing great things from you. Today, we really need to understand how to rebuild shattered dreams. There is so much negativity surrounding us. It's an achievement all within itself.

For me, the hardest thing I had to live with was loneliness. I felt that way until I healed from my past. It didn't matter that Jack and my children loved me. I still felt lonely. By healing from my past, the loneliness left me and I'm not afraid to be alone physically in the future. I know that I can live on my own very well and it won't hurt me unless I want it to.

Jack feels the same way. We are together because we want to be. I'm not with Jack because I need him. We choose to be with each other. Remember, a healthy relationship is when two people come together out of choice and not need. You're happier and your relationship is very healthy. You're friends because you want to be.

In my story, *Stones' Quest*, I show a family that has been split apart physically by war. They need to find each other and come together to stop the destruction of the galaxy. They must do it before the curse that's on their family destroys everything along with them.

They must unravel the mysteries to why their galaxy is falling apart. At one point, they have both sides of the war wanting to find them. One side thinks the protagonist is a traitor while the other side wants him because he can stop the war.

The protagonist must bring his family together to learn about the secrets that are destroying the galaxy. At the same time, he has a demon inside of him that he never wanted to face. I wrote the young adult series because I wanted to show the wrong and correct ways of facing yourself. Maybe, it will give someone ideas on how to deal with the uncertainties we live with these days. You'll have to read and find out how or if they succeed.

This book was a sacrifice for me to write. I hope you feel the price I paid has been beneficial for you. Even though I had healed long before I wrote this book, it wasn't enjoyable to actually stand in my shoes, asking my mind to give me back my feelings on how I felt growing up.

At first, Jack noticed my words change. My mind was going back to old patterns. I found myself repeating at night the nightmares of my youth. I was always moving myself in and out of my past. It wasn't easy and I so wanted to quit. Without me truly healing, I never could've written this book. I hope you find the price I paid for this information was worth it.

Remember, you can choose to be a survivor or a conqueror of your life. It's in your hands. The difference between the two is like night and day. To conquer your life, you'll love the results. Learn and enjoy the rewards.

About the Author

When growing up in rural Coalville, Utah, LaRene Ellis never planned to become a novelist, let alone one that could be internationally recognized. As a young child her life was carefree, filled with love, and normal by most standards, until her mother contracted cancer and passed away when LaRene was only four years of age. Her father, unable to take care of the three children, farmed them out to extended family and from that point her life would never be the same.

Those early impressionable years led to experiences that have molded the writer and created the insights that are reflected in her novels. The natural laws of life can be harsh for a four year old growing up in a challenging world and LaRene learned quickly to create her own positive environment within which to live. Inspiring experiences helped her acknowledge those around her who not only loved her, but also appreciated her for who she was, and recognized her latent talents. Little did she realize that life's natural laws would become such an influence in her writing.

In her youth, LaRene would reach out to those less fortunate to bring compassion and love into their lives—the giving of little gifts and the extending of kindnesses made a significant difference in those otherwise lonely lives. Reading books that inspired and uplifted, also helped her gain a sense of confidence and a realization of who she was.

Stones' Quest:
In Search of Its Master

For generations, the Ellisarius Galaxy enjoyed peace and prosperity as the Master of the Galaxy ruled with four pure white Stones of ultimate power. But three decades ago, the Stones were scattered and the Master disappeared . . .

Ghonllier is the best commander in the I-Force fleet, fighting valiantly in the galactic civil war against the evil Suzair the Great and the KOGN forces. But when the commander's ship rescues a young boy from a KOGN attack, Ghonllier is unprepared for the consequences, and the powerful secret the boy carries in his pocket. Now he must risk everything he holds dear as he races to find the answers that may save the galaxy.

Stones' Quest: In Search of its Master begins the tale of the great quest of the Stones. Filled with mystery and magic, spaceships and spies, the story chronicles an ongoing war between good and evil, and one man's journey to understand his own place in the universe.

ISBN: 0-9754622-0-2

All orders made on StonesQuest.com can be shipped to you within twenty-four hours. You can also order from Amazon or Barnes and Noble online or use the order form at the end of this book.

Stones' Quest: The Battles Begin

Centuries ago, a young sorceress fell in love, but not with the man chosen by her powerful father. Giving up everything she has, the lovers escape fleeing the moon and her father's hateful oppression. Or so they thought . . .

Battling KOGN and hiding from I-force, Ghonllier and his renegade crew continue their pursuit of the all-powerful Master Stones. Searching for a solution to reverse the curse destroying the galaxy, Ghonllier must confront his greatest fears foreseeing the untimely deaths of his closet friends and family. Meanwhile, Suzair the Great continues advancing his evil reign over an increasing number of systems in the galaxy. Can Ghonllier save the galaxy and prevent the deaths of those he loves? Or will he have to choose?

Stones' Quest: The Battles Begin continues the tale of the great quest of the Stones. Gaining more powers only adds to Ghonllier's inner turmoil. Teeming with suspense, the story illustrates powerful battles between the forces of good and evil, and one man's battles within himself.

ISBN: 0-9754622-1-0

All orders made on StonesQuest.com can be shipped to you within twenty-four hours. You can also order from Amazon or Barnes and Noble online or use the order form at the end of this book.

Stones' Quest: Redemption of the Curse

The Master Stones continue to unfold the mysteries of their plans for the galaxy. Have they left Ghonllier? Will Suzair the Great win because of it? Why does Bog want to find a baby that's important to Stacy and Adamite?

The third installment of the Stones' Quest series is riveted with action, mystery, adventure and romance. The battles between good and evil intensify as it comes down to the final chapter of the curse. Will Bog, the last sorcerer, win or will the Master Stones with it's chosen Master be the last one standing? They both can't stay in the galaxy. Most importantly, will the curse be stopped for good?

This and more will be answered in the next installment of the Stones' Quest Series. It will be out in the spring of 2008. Join the fan club at StonesQuest.com and you'll be first to learn the published date and price.

ISBN: 0-9754622-4-9

All orders made on StonesQuest.com can be shipped to you within twenty-four hours. You can also order from Amazon or Barnes and Noble online or use the order form at the end of this book.

Order Form

quantity			total price
_____	*How to Rebuild Shattered Dreams*	$14.95	_____
_____	*Stones' Quest: In Search of Its Master*	$19.95	_____
_____	*Stones' Quest: The Battles Begin*	$17.95	_____
_____	*Stones' Quest: Redemption of the Curse*	coming	_____

autographed copy (add $2 for each book) _____

tax (add 6.5% for orders to Utah addresses) _____

shipping (add $6 for first book and $2 for each additional) _____

grand total _____

Name _____

Address _____

_____

Credit card type _____ Number _____

Exp. date _____ Security code _____ Phone _____

Signature _____

Fax your order to 801-451-6008, or mail your check or money order along with this order form (or a photocopy of it) to:

Gathering Place Publishers, Inc.
P.O. Box 341
Kaysville, Utah 84037

Books can also be ordered from our web site HowToRebuildShatteredDreams.com or StonesQuest.com for faster delivery, or from Amazon or Barnes and Noble online.

Author's photograph provided by

Busath Photographers

701 East South Temple
Salt Lake City, Utah 84102

801-364-6645

www.busath.com